MALVERN COUNTRY

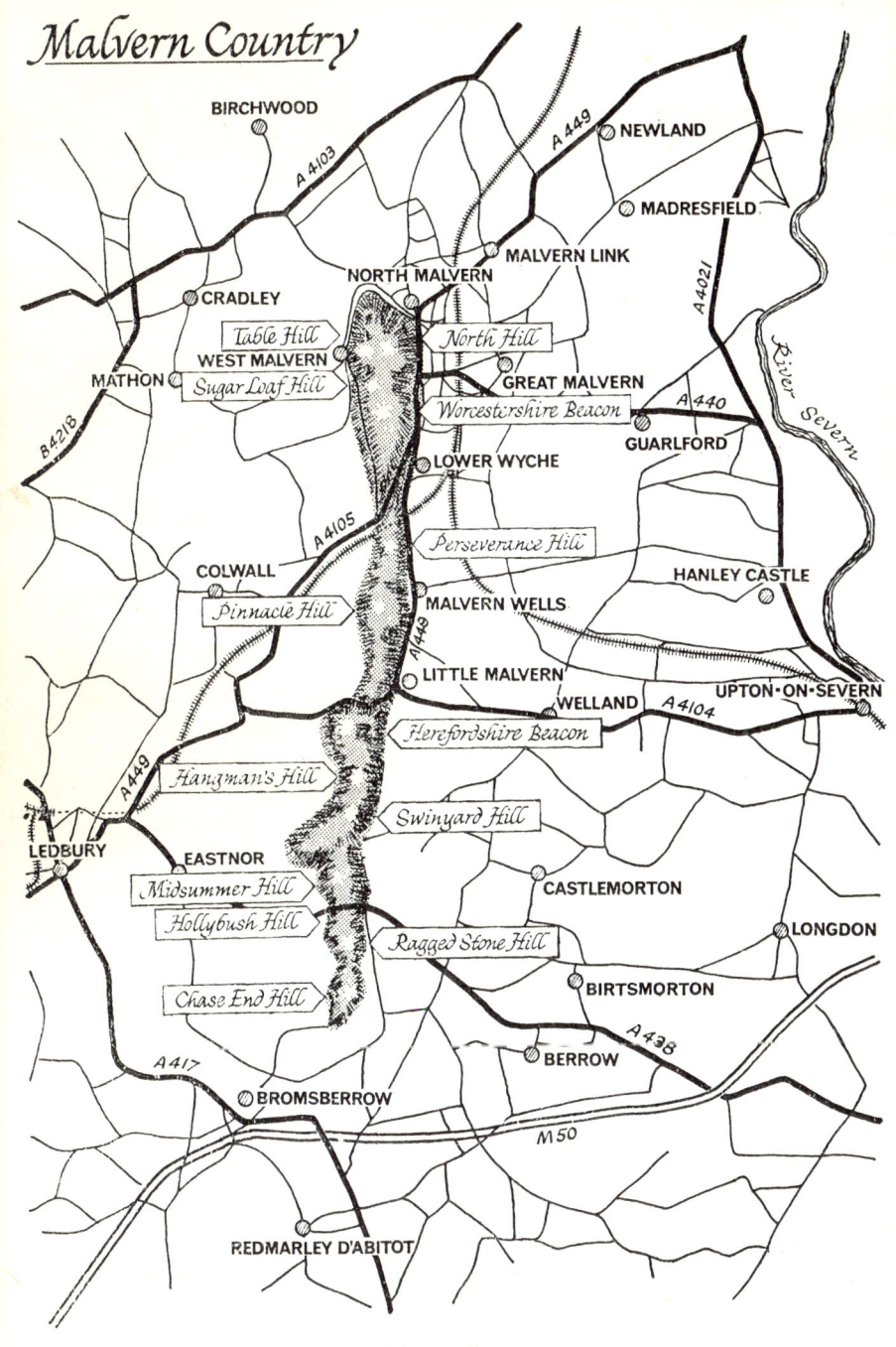

Malvern Country.

Malvern Country

VINCENT WAITE

★

WITH 16 PAGES OF PLATES
AND 2 MAPS

PHILLIMORE

First published by
J. M. DENT & SON LTD.
1968

This edition published by
PHILLIMORE & CO. LTD.
London and Chichester
Head Office: Shopwyke Hall,
Chichester, Sussex, England

ISBN 0 85033 333 4

Printed by Coasbyprint Limited,
Portsmouth, Hampshire

TO

M. L. W.

UXORI CARISSIMAE

Contents

Illustrations

xi

MAPS

Malvern Country, *frontispiece*
Geological map of the Malvern Hills, *page 4*

The relevant Ordnance Survey maps of the district are:
1-inch—sheet 143; 2½-inch—sheets SO 73 and SO 74

ACKNOWLEDGMENTS

Photograph 1 is by R. G. Honhold; photographs 2, 3, 4, 8, 9, 13, 16, 17, 18, 19, 20, 21, 22, 23 and 24 by M. L. Waite; 5, 6, 7, 10, 11, 12, 14, 15 and 25 by R. N. Cove. Photographs 11, 12 and 25 are by kind permission of Mrs Elgar Blake and the Trustees of the Elgar Birthplace.

A Select Bibliography

W. H. AINSWORTH: *Boscobel*

RALPH BLUMENAU: *A History of Malvern College*

A. H. BRIGHT: *New Light on Piers Plowman*

E. B. BROWNING: *Poetical Works*

ROBERT J. BUCKLEY: *Sir Edward Elgar*

JOAN BULMAN: *Jenny Lind*

C. F. SEVERN BURROW: *A Little City Set on a Hill*

JOHN CHAMBERS: *A General History of Malvern*

FLORENCE CONVERSE: *Long Will*

CANON A. C. DEANE: *A Short Account of Great Malvern Priory Church*

DANIEL DEFOE: *A Tour Through England and Wales*

WILLIAM DREGHORN: *The Malverns and May Hill*

VERA L. EDMINSON: *Ancient Misericords in the Priory Church*

JOHN EVELYN: *Diary*

DOROTHEA FARQUHARSON: *The Church of St Michael and All Angels, Ledbury*

CELIA FIENNES: *Journeys* (ed. Christopher Morris)

H. L. V. FLETCHER: *Herefordshire*

JOHN FORSTER: *Life of Charles Dickens*

H. C. A. GAUNT: *Two Exiles*

CHARLES F. GRINDROD: *The Shadow of the Ragged Stone*

R. B. GRINDROD: *Malvern Past and Present* and *The Compressed Air Bath*

J. M. GULLY: *The Water Cure in Chronic Disease*

L. A. HAMAND: *The Ancient Windows of Great Malvern Priory Church*

GLYNNE HASTINGS: *A Short History of the Three Counties Agricultural Society*

F. T. S. HOUGHTON: *Little Guide to Worcestershire*

JOHN H. INGRAM: *Elizabeth Barrett Browning*

JOSEPH LEECH: *Three Weeks in Wet Sheets . . .*

J. LEES-SMITH: *Worcestershire*

xiii

JOHN LELAND: *Itinerary*

W. H. McMENEMY: *Water Doctors of Malvern*

DIANA M. McVEAGH: *Edward Elgar*

BASIL MAINE: *Elgar, His Life and Works*

JOHN MASEFIELD: *Collected Poems* and *Grace Before Ploughing*

ARTHUR MEE: *Herefordshire* and *Worcestershire*

CATHERINE MOODY: *The Silhouette of Malvern*

T. NASH: *Worcestershire*

J. NOAKE: *Guide to Worcestershire*

JAMES NOTT: *Church and Monastery of 'Moche Malverne'* and
Malvern Priory Church

HESKETH PEARSON: *Bernard Shaw*

R. W. POCOCK and T. H. WHITEHEAD: *British Regional
Geology: the Welsh Borderland*

MRS RICHARD POWELL: *Edward Elgar: Memories of a Variation*

W. H. REED: *Elgar* (Master Musicians) and *Elgar As I Knew Him*

L. T. C. ROLT: *Worcestershire*

A. P. ROWE: *One Story of Radar*

J. H. SHORTHOUSE: *John Inglesant*

BRIAN S. SMITH: *A History of Malvern*

FINOLA LADY SOMERS and ELIZABETH HERVEY-BATHURST:
Eastnor Castle

M. SOUTHALL: *Description of Malvern*

W. S. SYMONDS: *Hanley Castle* and *Malvern Chase*

REV. PHILIP B. THORBURN: *A Short History of and Guide to
Mathon Church*

G. O. TREVELYAN: *The Life and Letters of Lord Macaulay*

REV. J. WEBSTER: *Malvern and its Environs*

HENRY W. WELLS: *The Vision of Piers Plowman*

LEONARD J. WILLS: *Worcestershire*

DR J. WILSON: *A Practical Treatise on the Cure of Diseases by Water*

PERCY M. YOUNG: *Elgar, O.M., Letters of Edward Elgar* and
Letters to Nimrod from Edward Elgar (Ed.)

Elgar Centenary Sketches
R.R.E. Offers Opportunities

Preface

THE Malverns and the surrounding countryside form one of the
most beautiful, historic and interesting districts in England. It is an
impressive experience just to climb the hills and to look over a
landscape where may be seen as many as fifteen counties, three
cathedrals, six abbeys and priories, and as many historic battlefields; but it is hoped that this book will add to the pleasure by
tracing the outline of the story which lies behind what can be
seen. The Malverns are made up of some of the oldest rocks in the
world, and one curious result of bringing prehistory and history
together is that we revise our sense of time, and after reading of
strata formed here over four hundred millions of years ago, the
events of history seem almost like yesterday, and we realize, for
example, that Charles the Second's visit to Madresfield before the
battle of Worcester was less than five seventy-year lifetimes ago.

As A. L. Rowse has aptly put it, 'history isn't something that is
dead and done with: it is something that is alive and all around
us . . . in things we see before our eyes', and this book sets out
not only to recapture for the ordinary reader some of the history
of Malvern's past, but also to convey something of the atmosphere of its present, which together give the district its distinctive character. It is planned so that it can be read with equal
interest, I hope, by both walkers and motorists, and both before
and after a visit to the district so that landscape, buildings and
people can all be seen and recalled with greater understanding
and deeper appreciation.

Many authoritative books on the history of Malvern country
both in fact and fiction are now out of print or not easily accessible
to the general reader. As a special feature of this book I have
therefore included a number of quotations from a variety of
authors so that they form something of a selective anthology of
what has been memorably written about these hills and their
surroundings, about their history and their people.

V. W.

Acknowledgments

I owe a special debt of gratitude to Mrs Carice Elgar Blake, Sir Edward Elgar's daughter, for her ready advice and help when I was writing Chapter IV; and to the late John Masefield, Poet Laureate, for his generous permission to quote from his works, and for his friendly interest expressed in characteristically kindly letters. I have also received valuable help from my wife and R. N. Cove, Esq., who provided many of the photographs for this book; from Mrs Colston Waite, who helped with the typescript; and from A. W. Coysh, Esq., who wrote the geological sketch of the Malverns.

Among others who have given me generous and ready help in obtaining information and material I have to thank George Allen & Unwin; the Society of Authors; the Librarian, Balliol College, Oxford; G. Bell & Sons; Ralph Blumenau, Esq.; Cambridge University Press; Alban Claughton, Esq.; *Country Life*; Mrs Kathleen Dawes; J. M. Dent & Sons; *Gloucestershire Countryside*; Glynne Hastings, Esq.; R. G. Honhold, Esq.; G. B. Honour, Esq.; the *Malvern Gazette*; the *Marble Archer* (Schweppes Ltd); Methuen & Co.; Miss Catherine Moody; Novello & Co.; N. H. Parker, Esq., and the staff of the Malvern Public Library; Mrs Mary Quartley; the Director of the Royal Radar Establishment; George Sayer, Esq.; Alan Webb, Esq.; and the Rev. P. G. Young.

CHAPTER ONE

The Ebb and Flow of History

FOR nearly nine miles the Malvern Hills thrust a dramatic serrated outline skywards as they rise abruptly out of the surrounding countryside, forming a partial boundary between the counties of Worcestershire and Herefordshire. The general north to south direction of the range is slightly modified by the westerly bulges of the Herefordshire Beacon and Chase End Hill, and the ridge of the hills is remarkably narrow, besides being loftier in the north than in the south, although its undulations produce altogether some twenty distinct peaks throughout its length. Some are pointed or otherwise obvious; others are broader and less conspicuous. Three main roads cross the hills: one through the Wyche links Great Malvern and Colwall; another by Wynd's Point is the main road from Great Malvern to Ledbury and Hereford; and the third, the Tewkesbury to Ledbury road, passes between Midsummer Hill and Ragged Stone Hill. Other tracks or rough roads cross the hills—e.g. between the Herefordshire Beacon and Swinyard Hill, and through the passage between Ragged Stone Hill and Chase End Hill; but these are more suitable and more accessible for the pedestrian than a vehicle.

Dr Grindrod pointed out that on the northern part of the range only a few of the peaks have names and they are apparently modern, but south of the Herefordshire Beacon the hills bear names which seem to be of some antiquity. Starting from the north, the range comprises North Hill, Table Hill, Sugar Loaf Hill, Worcestershire Beacon, Perseverance Hill, Pinnacle Hill, Herefordshire Beacon (or Camp Hill), Hangman's Hill, Swinyard Hill, Midsummer Hill (and Hollybush Hill), Ragged Stone Hill, Chase End Hill (or the Gloucestershire Beacon).

The origin of the name 'Malvern' has been the subject of a good deal of argument and some fanciful speculation. There is general agreement that the first syllable is derived from the Celtic word *Moel* meaning 'bald'. It is the second syllable which has provoked the controversy. Some trace it to *Wern* meaning 'alders' (i.e. the bald hill with the alders); others suggest *Varn* or 'seat of judgment'; or *Hafren*, 'of the Severn'. One writer goes as far as to claim that the name refers to *Malvhina*, a Celtic princess. The generally accepted modern theory derives the name from *Moel* and *Bryn* meaning the 'Bare Hill'. Before the Norman Conquest the name is spelt 'Maelfern'; in Domesday the place appears as 'Malferna'; and in later times the names 'Malveselle' and 'Malveshill' are also found. Celia Fiennes spells the name 'Mauborn', and later with characteristic inconsistency 'Maubern'. A quarter of a century later Defoe writes it as 'Maulvern' and gives as an alternative 'Mauvern'.

From the heights of the range there are views which deserve all the superlatives which have been given them by enthusiastic writers, and it is perhaps no exaggeration to say that 'for extent all round they can hardly be equalled in Great Britain, and perhaps not in many other countries, except from very high and favourably placed mountains'; and the Malverns, of course, provide ideal walking country. They offer the gentlest of climbs which reward the walker with 'almost alpine views', and there are also a number of steeper paths which provide more strenuous exercise. The hills are criss-crossed by something like twenty-six miles of footpaths over grassy uplands which have the inestimable advantage of drying out for the climber shortly after even the heaviest rainstorm. Colours here are infinitely various throughout the year, changing with the season. In spring time the vivid green is offset by may, bluebells, wild cherries, broom and the pink froth of blossom in distant orchards; and especially around Redmarley by a wealth of cowslips and wild daffodils. Summer brings gorse, purple loose-strife and willow herb, foxgloves, honeysuckle, violets, wild thyme and sudden patches of pale blue where that daintiest of wild flowers, the harebell, covers the turf. Then follows the rich glowing russet of the bracken in the autumn, with the haze of the Herefordshire hop-yards; and in the winter there is the glossy green of holly bushes which stand out even more clearly if snow has come to the hills.

The views of the Malvern Hills from a distance are remarkable, too, with a characteristic beauty of their own. Seen from the

eastern side they seem almost mountainous as they rise sheer and
sharp from the plain with an outline like the heaving shape of
some vast prehistoric monster. From the west, with the greater
upward tilt of the land on that side, they appear less high than
they really are, and their outline is less stark as they sink gradually
into Herefordshire with undulating swells and low wooded
knolls. One feature of the Malverns has often been remarked
upon—the characteristic bluish-purple colour which they show
when seen from a distance, and which gives them an atmosphere
of brooding mystery and infinite age. This is indeed a land which
has known the ebb and flow of history from far distant ages, and
when you stand on 'the rudimentary ridge of the Malverns' you
are on some of the oldest rocks in the world, where geologists
have often sought to discover the secrets of our distant past.

Secrets there still are, but the geologists have patiently pieced
together at least part of the story. We know that some of these
ancient rocks forming the backbone of the Malverns were
originally formed by volcanic action, for it is possible in places to
see the kind of ashes and fragments that are blown out from a
volcanic vent as molten lava wells up from the depths, and flows
out on the earth's surface to cool and form solid rock. Some have
cooled more slowly below the surface to form crystalline rocks,
and all of them have since been subjected to intense pressures so
that chemical changes have taken place and produced new
minerals. The rocks in any of the northern Malvern quarries,
particularly at the freshly broken surfaces, show the tiny shining
plates of mica, white and pink felspar, and hard colourless quartz
which when washed down by rivers in its weathered state gives
us the sand of our seashores. The physical results of pressure are
also apparent; some of the rocks split or flake easily into thin
layers, and in others the darker minerals occur in curving lines
which show the folding. These rocks are known to geologists as
pre-Cambrian rocks, older than most of the rocks of Wales to the
west (hence the name), and much older than those of the Severn
valley to the east.

For a long period of time they must have remained as a rugged
island in a surrounding sea, subject to the eroding action of frost
and rain. The Cambrian and Silurian rocks formed by the materials
washed down from the hills are seen to the west—the Cambrian
in the southern area west of Hollybush Hill, Ragged Stone Hill

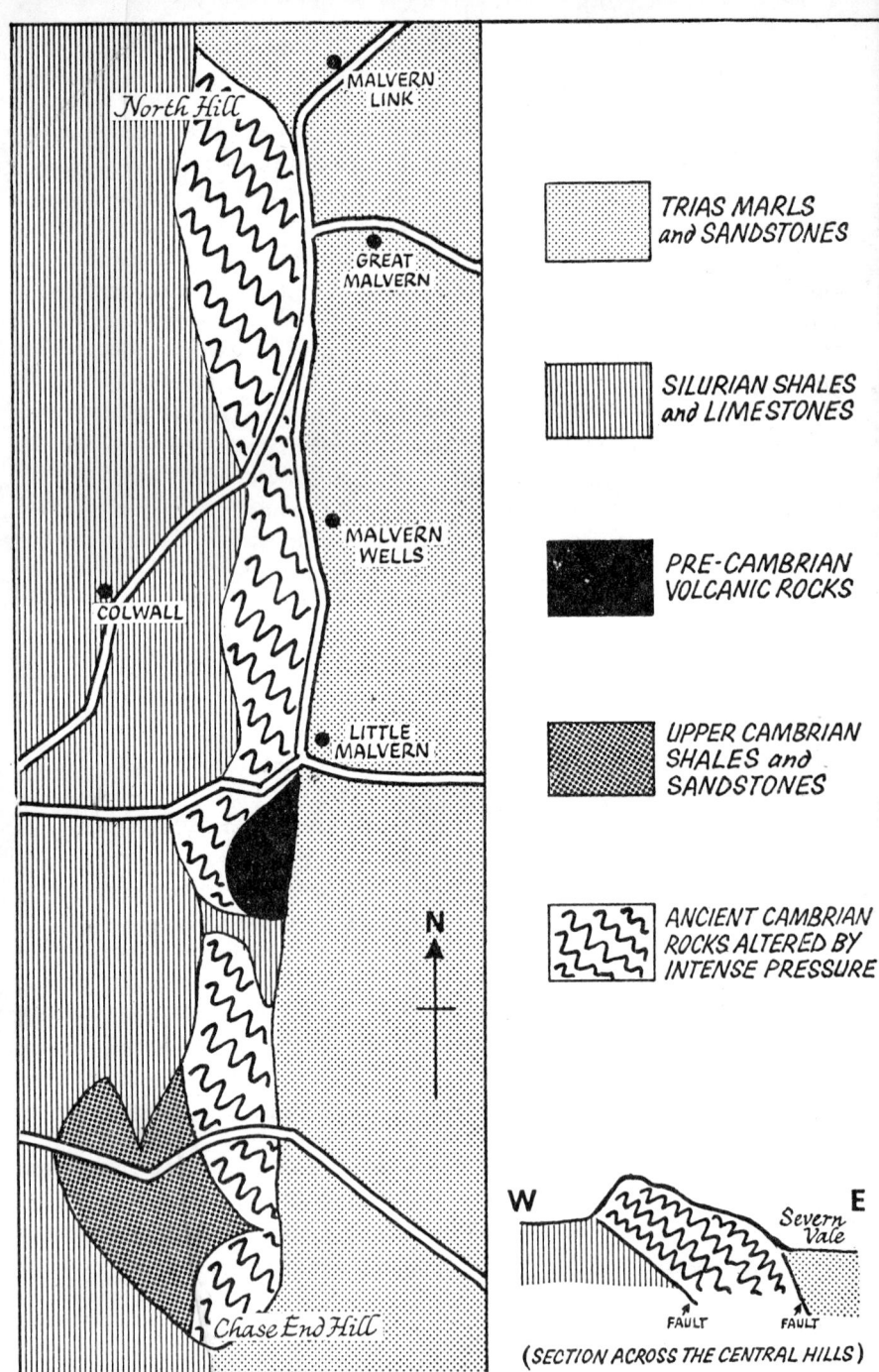

Legend:

- TRIAS MARLS and SANDSTONES
- SILURIAN SHALES and LIMESTONES
- PRE-CAMBRIAN VOLCANIC ROCKS
- UPPER CAMBRIAN SHALES and SANDSTONES
- ANCIENT CAMBRIAN ROCKS ALTERED BY INTENSE PRESSURE

North Hill

MALVERN LINK

GREAT MALVERN

MALVERN WELLS

COLWALL

LITTLE MALVERN

N

Chase End Hill

W — E

Severn Vale

FAULT   FAULT

(SECTION ACROSS THE CENTRAL HILLS)

Geological Map of the Malvern Hills.

and Chase End Hill; and the Silurian along the rest of the western slopes. There are fossils, remains of small sea creatures, to be found in all the sediments, and there must have been periods when the waters were clear, for in the Silurian rocks are great banks of coral, formed under conditions similar to those which exist today along the coast of Queensland in Australia, where masses of coral form the Great Barrier Reef. Traces of the shingle beach of the Silurian sea can still be seen in Gullet Quarry between Swinyard Hill and Midsummer Hill. The coral limestones are hard, and stand out as a sweeping ridge known as the Ridgeway, which is clearly seen from Herefordshire Beacon.

After most of these sedimentary rocks had been laid down under water there was another period of great earth movement. The pressures in the Malvern area were from the east, piling up the oldest rocks of the ridge towards the later rocks which lie to the west. Indeed at Herefordshire Beacon they were forced over the Silurian rocks which now lie beneath them. This is why the slopes to the west of the Malverns are gentler and more irregular than those to the east where the land is lower. The soft marly rocks of the Trias forming the Severn Vale were laid down later in a shallow sea, and they lie against the hills along the line of a long crack (or fault) in the earth's surface—the Malvern Fault—marked by the steep eastern slopes. During the Ice Age, great masses of ice pushed down from the north on either side of the Malvern Hills. They may or may not have covered the actual hills, but they certainly joined up in the southern area, because when the ice began to melt a lake formed for a time to the west of the hills. The sands and gravels left behind when it drained away can still be seen in shallow pits at South End near Mathon.

By now the scene had been set for its occupation by primitive man, but although Nature has thus left the earliest story of Malvern's history imprinted in rock for the geologist to read, at least in part, its later prehistory is lost in a mist of shadowy conjecture. At that early period, when all the surrounding land was covered by a dense tangle of forest interspersed with swamps and the flooding of a Severn which was then a tidal estuary, the hills must have provided better trackways and safer higher territory for those early races who went in 'continual fear and danger of violent death', and whose 'life was solitary, poor, nasty, brutish and short'. The surviving camps on Herefordshire Beacon and on Midsummer Hill must have been made in an early and perhaps simpler form by some of these primitive people, and the 'British' Camp may well date back to the Iron Age. Unfortunately excavations on these sites have yielded few conclusive clues in the shape of tools or weapons, and even the contours and construction of the camps must have been considerably modified by successive generations. The strategic position of the Malverns, towering above the disputed land to the west, inevitably made them an important outpost against the fierce warlike Celtic tribes of the Welsh Marches, and the tradition of a defensive stand made by Caractacus against the Romans on the Herefordshire Beacon [1] may well have some basis in fact.

In 1650, when a labourer, Thomas Tailer,[2] was digging a ditch around his cottage at Burstner's Cross near the present site of the British Camp Hotel, he unearthed 'a coronet or bracelet of gold, set with precious stones, of a size to be drawn over the arm and sleeve'. The simple countryman took the treasure to Gloucester and sold it to a jeweller there for £37. The jeweller in turn sold it to a London goldsmith for £250, and he disposed of the stones alone for £1,500—a remarkable example of a capital gain. It has been suggested that this richly embellished gold ornament may well have been the coronet of a young British prince; if so, its discovery near the Herefordshire Beacon is of special interest.

Nearly two hundred years later, an urn was found in the quarry beside the same site of the British Camp Hotel. It contained some two hundred coins, and a further search revealed a red-coloured earthen pot with another fifty coins. They were carefully examined and were found to bear the imprint of five Roman emperors reigning within the period of A.D. 286–311. In spite of its local interest the finding of this treasure trove does not prove that the Romans made much inroad on the 'vast wilderness of Malvern', as William of Malmesbury described it eight centuries later. They would be much more likely to keep to the comparative safety and comfort they had organized at nearby Gloucester.

When the Roman occupation ended in 410, Britain had enjoyed a degree of peace and prosperity for a period of something like three and a half centuries. Accustomed to the protection of Roman arms, the Britons probably had lost something

---

[1] *See* page 84.
[2] There is an entry of his burial in the Colwall parish records.

of their ancient warlike spirit when the merciless hordes of Saxons, Angles and Jutes descended on the shores of England amid a welter of greed and bloodshed. The newcomers were as ruthless as they were fearless, but fortunately those who had fled to the Malvern Hills or had hidden in Malvern Forest were sufficiently far from the main tide of history at this period to know only the edge of it as it ebbed and flowed around them.

After the Saxon conquest was consolidated it was the turn of the Saxons themselves to face an invader. The Danes began to harry the coasts, and plunder and slaughter were brought to the very threshold of Malvern country when parties of these new marauders began to sail up the River Severn, spreading terror and destruction as they went. According to Leland on one such raid they attacked and destroyed the monastery at neighbouring Deerhurst in Gloucestershire. One monk escaped—'Werstanus fledde thens, as it is sayde, to Malverne'. This story has given rise to a legend connected with the earliest ecclesiastical history of Malvern and illustrated in four of the most beautiful of the priory's fifteenth-century windows in the north clerestory of the choir.

The first window, starting from the left, represents against a background of the Malvern Hills four angels blessing the site and holding the corner-stones of a hillside chapel for 'Sanctus Werstanus Martir'. The next window shows the same angels dressed in priestly robes consecrating the completed chapel with all the appropriate ecclesiastical accompaniments of the rite—cross, bell, censer and holy water sprinkler. In the third window an oversize figure of Edward the Confessor hands a sealed charter, not to St Werstan himself, but to a diminutive ecclesiastical figure labelled 'Willm' Edwardus', possibly Werstan's representative. The fourth window vividly portrays Werstan's martyrdom. A pair of purposeful-looking ruffians with long two-handed swords stand outside the chapel and one of them is shown hacking at Werstan's head as he imprudently looks out of the window. Below, the same two miscreants are shown waiting with scourges to belabour three innocent singing clerks who are chanting inside the chapel.

Although Werstan is thus immortalized in stained glass, it is difficult to connect his story with the foundation of Malvern Priory. The oldest documents make no mention of him, and indeed his name is unknown to any calendar of English saints. Details of the origin of the priory are in fact impossible to trace with any certainty because there are several accounts which cannot be reconciled. The most that we can say is that although some kind of religious community may have existed in the neighbourhood during the time of Edward the Confessor yet the true priory of Great Malvern was founded after the Norman Conquest.

After the Conquest it was only natural that William should reward those who had shared with him the risks of the invasion, and land filched from English landowners provided suitable booty. A rich, comfortably ensconced Saxon thane like Brictric [1] was deprived of twenty thousand acres, and there were many others who had to hand over their landed possessions to doughty Norman warriors or, bitterest pill of all, to lowlier Norman upstarts like William's cook and his apothecary. English prelates with the substantial landed endowments of the Church were treated with special ruthlessness. With one exception all the bishops lost their sees and were replaced by Normans. The exception was Wulfstan [2] of Worcester, the last of the Anglo-Saxon saints, and one who was traditionally most closely connected with the foundation of Malvern Priory.

William of Normandy, of all people, could hardly be described as sentimental or scrupulous, and there must have been a good reason for this exception made in the case of the diocese of Worcester. William was a shrewd judge of character, and Wulfstan was a man even he could not fail to admire and respect. The bishop was a diligent administrator, and he combined in some extraordinary way an insistence on rigid discipline with an infinite capacity for friendship and happiness. Monks who arrived late for services were punished by smart blows from a stick he kept for this purpose; and he is said to have disapproved so strongly of the custom of wearing very long hair adopted by the vicious youths of the court that he never lost an opportunity of cutting off their locks with the scissors he always carried with him—but no one seems to have borne him any animosity for these disconcerting foibles. Strictly abstemious himself, he delighted in offering liberal hospitality to others; and although

[1] *See* page 23.
[2] Also spelt 'Wulstan' and 'Wolstan'.

showing charitable tolerance to most human frailties, he practised a blameless purity in his own life. This was the man who according to William of Malmesbury influenced a hermit, Aldwin, who founded the Malvern Priory:

> There was one Aldwin, a monk, who with a single companion named Guido lived as a recluse in that very densely wooded Chase which is called Malvern. After long struggles of conscience Guido considered it absolutely necessary, as the shortest path to glory, to visit Jerusalem and see the Lord's sepulchre, or meet a blessed death by the hands of the Saracens. Aldwin was disposed to follow his example but first consulted his spiritual adviser Wulfstan. The prelate dissuaded him and cooled his ardour by saying, 'Do not, I beseech thee, Aldwin, go anywhere, but remain in your place. Believe me, you would wonder if you knew what I know; how much God is about to perform through you in that place.' The monk having heard this departed, and now remained firm in purpose and soothed every sorrow by the hope of the prophecy.

Wulfstan's prediction was soon fulfilled; in a short space of time Aldwin had gathered thirty monks around him to form the nucleus of the new Benedictine priory which, according to Worcester's Monastic Annals, 'was founded in 1085'. From then until its dissolution in 1541 the history of Malvern Priory (together with that of the Forest [1]) is the story of Malvern.

Below the Werstan windows already described are four others showing some possible sources of what must have been considerable endowments for the priory, for although comparatively modest in size the monastery had an impressive collection of buildings which would have entailed equally impressive expenses. About the beginning of the fifteenth century a magnificent timbered Guesten-House was built for the accommodation of travellers; and even after the Dissolution this survived as a noble barn until 1841 when, with barbaric insensitivity, it was wantonly torn down to make more room for the water-cure patients. 'It is certain that abbeys and priories covenanted in their foundations to have their gates ever open to receive the poor,' wrote one chronicler, 'and we see what Great Malvern did in sustaining these necessities.' Malvern Priory was always renowned for its

[1] Related in Chapter Two.

charity and for its hospitality to those wayfarers who braved the strenuous tracks over the heights of the hills or risked the dangers lurking beside the winding paths through Malvern Forest.

One interesting source of income for the priory was the manufacture of encaustic tiles which obviously grew to a considerable industry. More than one thousand of these tiles can still be seen inside the priory church, and many more can be found in other churches over a wide area. During the nineteenth century, workmen digging over what was formerly priory land uncovered one of the monastic kilns still in a remarkably good state of preservation and containing several tiles similar to those inside the church today.

Among the succession of priors who for some four and a half centuries followed Aldwin, some were meritorious, some inadequate, and at least one, the profligate William of Ledbury, was entirely disreputable. This notorious William was elected prior at the end of the thirteenth century, was then deposed when his behaviour became too openly scandalous to be either ignored or hidden, was later reinstated and then deposed again. This extraordinary chapter in the history of the priory was the result of the monastery's link with Westminster Abbey at the time of its foundation, or at least from a very early date. As Malvern thus refused to accept the authority of the bishops of Worcester, this led to a whole series of triangular quarrels involving the priory, Westminster and Worcester which culminated in this unseemly scandal of the 'William of Ledbury affair'. It is pleasanter to record, however, that the immediate successor of Aldwin himself was the saintly scholar Walcher of Lorraine, of whom William of Malmesbury said that 'to disbelieve him is to do an injustice to religion'. Walcher's coffin slab is still preserved in St Anne's Chapel in the church; its inscription consists of some mongrel dog-Latin verse, typical of the period.

In his *Reflections Relative to the Malvern Hills*, E. M. Rudd includes a somewhat idealized reconstruction of the Malvern countryside as it would have looked during this Norman period of its history:

> I see beneath these hills, instead of this diversified, cheerful scene of cultivation, a vast straggling forest, interspersed with heathy pastures, with much fewer dwellings visible, chiefly huts and cottages, and here and there a

Malvern Ridge

The Herefordshire Beacon

The ancient hunting-lodge at Colwall

The Priory gateway

Malvern Spa doctors:
Dr James Wilson

Dr James Gully (a 'Spy'
cartoon)

The Malvern water-cure: the 'Douche'

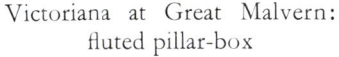

Victoriana at Great Malvern: fluted pillar-box

Victoriana at Great Malvern: cast-iron capitals in the railway station

The Malvern Holy Well in a more gracious age

Elgar and Shaw at the Malvern Festival

Elgar at Forli

Great Malvern from St Ann's Road

great man's castle bosomed in trees—the wide forest scene having a rich and noble but far more lonely aspect. Archers at a distance appear and disappear among the trees, traversing the Chase in quest of deer. Solitude, nevertheless, strongly characterizes the scene. I have before me the grey Priory and its conventual buildings. Its bell sounds among the rocks. Cowled monks walk among the thick alder clumps below. Some are setting out on a spiritual visit to the peasants, or to the household of some baron. Others return with water from the Holy Well two miles distant. Some are here upon the hills. One sits reading among rocks and tangled bushes; and two or three are above near the summit, looking down on the expanse below.

About the spot where we are now sitting I figure to myself a pair of the reverend brethren strolling calmly after their vespers on some sober summer eve, discoursing in serene, lofty, moralizing mood on some subject friendly to pious hope; and then with a sacred serenity of soul going down in twilight through the bushes to their place of repose.

Although this would perhaps be too reassuring a picture of the monks' innocent activities at some periods in the history of the priory, no doubt throughout its best years the monks of Malvern lived by the Rule of their distinguished Benedictine Order; and in a bleak, brutal, pitiless world kept alive the shining light of scholarship, prayer, hospitality, charity and healing. They gave shelter to saint and penitent, student and outcast, artist and artisan, writer and musician; and in obedience to their founder's command they laboured in turn with their hands at menial tasks in humility of spirit.

Following the usual pattern, the main monastery buildings at Malvern faced south, including the cloisters, so that the place where the monks spent most of their waking hours when they were not in church was open to as much sunshine as possible. The close proximity of church, cloister, refectory and dormitory must have severely tested that development of saintliness in communal living which was such an important aspect of St Benedict's Rule. Another essential feature of monastic life was of course the ordered, regular sequence of worship provided by a complicated series of services. The Malvern monks' day would be reckoned from sunrise to sunset, and they fitted into the twenty-four hours no less than seven services from Matins to Compline, as well as meals, chapter meetings to settle business, study, work in infirmary, guest house or garden or at more menial tasks, and their few hours of broken sleep.

It was an orderly, peaceful way of life, and it must have had a considerable attraction for those who preferred to make a total surrender of their lives rather than face the undeniably brutal realities of ordinary everyday life in that harsh age. And remote as Malvern may have seemed, echoes of the anarchy, warfare and misery of King Stephen's misrule must have been heard even there when 'the fairest regions were devastated with rapine and fire and in what had once been the most fertile of fatherlands almost all the food was destroyed'. It was cruelly ironic—but inevitable—that it should be the reign of Stephen, 'a mild man and good', which was 'nineteen long winters' when 'Christ and his Saints slept', and the monks of Malvern could hardly fail to tremble with the worst forebodings when the King marched his army through Worcester to attack Dudley Castle, and when later the city was pillaged and burnt, first by the pitiless Matilda and then by the avenging forces of Stephen himself.

During the fourteenth century the Malvern Hills were immortalized in English literature by William Langland, the supposed author of *The Vision of Piers Plowman*. They form the gentle, almost tender, introductory background to the later satire and indignation of this 'epic of Christian justice', as Arthur Bryant has described it, for it opens with a haunting description of Langland sleeping on the hills:

> In a summer season when soft was the sun,
> I dressed me in a shepherd's smock
> As though I a shepherd were,
> In the habit of a hermit, though of no holy life,
> I wandered wide about this world, wonders to see.
> In a May morning on Malvern Hills
> A strange thing befell me, a fairy vision methought,
> I was weary of wandering and went me to rest
> Under a broad bank beside a stream,
> And as I lay and leaned and looked upon the water,
> I slumbered in a sleep, so pleasantly it sounded.

A long tradition makes Langland the author of this great poem, but practically all we know about him is conjectural or based on fragments of information he himself gives. One fifteenth-century manuscript notes that his father was Eustace de Rokayle, who is known to have held land from the Despensers of Hanley Castle and who must often have been in these parts. If this information about his paternity is correct Langland may well have been his illegitimate son born about 1332 of some peasant woman living near Longland, a modern equivalent of Langland, in the parish of Colwall. The author of the poem repeatedly tells us that his name is William, with the nickname 'Long Will' on account of his height, and he records that his father and his friends provided for his education, most probably at Great Malvern Priory.

He later lived in Cornhill, London, earning a beggarly living as a kind of chantry clerk, singing dirges at the funerals of the well to do. Although he was tonsured he could have taken only minor orders because he was married to a woman called Kitte and had a daughter Calote. In spite of his poverty he appears to have been fiercely independent, silently angry at the pride of the rich, silently sorrowing at the miseries of the poor, and with a resentful sense of inferiority which his possible illegitimacy might explain. 'It requires no great stretch of imagination', writes Skeat, 'to picture to ourselves the tall gaunt figure of Long Will, in his long robes and with his shaven head, striding along Cornhill, saluting no man by the way, minutely observant of the gay dresses to which he paid no outward reverence'.

Piers Plowman is a great poem by any standards, as anyone will agree who reads even only a part of it in one of the modern versions by Nevill Coghill or Henry W. Wells. It presents a brilliant, evocative picture of fourteenth-century characters, life and work which makes a startling and salutary pendant to his contemporary Chaucer's tolerant, genial satire. Ploughmen, friars, bishops, lawyers, burgesses, cooks and taverners—all crowd into the great canvas of Langland's

> Fair field, full of folk . . . of all manner of men,
> The poor and the rich, working and idling.

He can pass easily from the hushed calm of the Malvern Hills to the harsh clamour of the crowded city, and some of the realism, like the confessions of the Seven Deadly Sins, is brutally frank enough to jolt even a hardened modern reader who prides himself on being unshockable. Yet together with all this there are also lofty and lyrical passages which, says the French critic Legouis, 'like gems . . . would gain by extraction from their matrix', and would form an admirable anthology.

Since the poem as a whole is such a bitter satire on the contrast between rich and poor, it is not surprising that it had such a popular success with those who lacked the advantages of high birth and wealth. This is evident from the number of manuscripts of the poem which were made, and from the allusions to it in the works of the following two centuries. Beyond the satire of *Piers Plowman*, however, lies the dreamer's earnest quest for the Good Life and for the secret of Salvation, although it must be confessed that the consolations of religion which he offers are somewhat gloomily represented, and it is significant that the dreamer awakes weeping bitterly after his ninth and last dream.

Florence Converse's novel *Long Will* reconstructs a convincing fictional representation of this colourful age around the eponymous hero William Langland and other contemporary figures like Chaucer, Wat Tyler, John Wycliff and Richard the Second. It captures, with uncommon sincerity and sensitive feeling, the vigour and vitality of fourteenth-century England and opens with a Prologue set in the Malvern Hills where the young Langland is wandering restlessly, planning his poem. In the concluding Epilogue, Long Will has returned once again to his native hills and lies dying in the priory's infirmary, watched over by an old monk who remembered him as a boy.

During the fifteenth century there was a sweeping reconstruction of the priory church, and for many years the hills must have echoed and re-echoed to the sound of hammer and winch, saw and chisel, axe and adze, as masons, carpenters and labourers set about raising a new tower, and rebuilt the sanctuary, chancel and choir aisles all in the new Perpendicular style—that national variation of Gothic which was virtually started in Gloucester Cathedral. The massive Norman pillars of the nave were left, but the width of the north aisle was increased, although the position of the cloisters against the south wall made it impossible to do the same on that side. By 1460 this great task of rebuilding was completed, and on 30th July the Bishop of Worcester arrived at the priory to consecrate the new church's seven altars. He was received 'with the ringing of bells, and passed the night with the ministering clergy and their servants at the expense of the house'.

The last five years of this rebuilding was carried on after the beginning of the tragic Wars of the Roses, but the miseries of this pitiless civil strife were sufficiently distant from Malvern to allow the monks to continue with their task of filling their church's windows with some of the most beautiful stained glass in the country. Then the tide of the war flowed dangerously near in 1471. At Tewkesbury, only a few miles away, the Yorkists fought and defeated the forces of Queen Margaret of Anjou, the 'She-wolf of France', and her luckless young son Prince Edward was overtaken as he fled through the 'Bloody Meadow' and was mercilessly butchered as he pitifully begged for quarter.[1]

It is difficult to realize that it was less than eighty years after the Bishop of Worcester's visit to consecrate the altars of the rebuilt priory when tragedy and destruction came to the monastery. This is not the place to discuss how far the accusations of idleness, vice and worldliness brought against some of the monasteries were true at that particular time when Henry the Eighth was determined to hasten his divorce from Katherine of Aragon. What is certain is that not even the undoubted contributions which these monasteries made to culture, learning and charitable works could have in any way influenced the King's determination to do without Rome, and to confiscate all the revenues of the monasteries for himself. Malvern must have suspected the worst when in 1536 the smaller monasteries were suppressed. Two years later the Prior wrote beseechingly to Thomas Cromwell saying they thought it 'expedient to ask the King's pleasure how they should order themselves'. At that time the priory's reputation stood high; the worst charge that was brought against its monks was that they held certain holy relics in excessive veneration—a harmless failing, one would have thought. Even the strictly Protestant Bishop Latimer of Worcester made a last despairing effort to prevent its destruction. His highly commendable idea was to preserve at least two or three monasteries in every county 'not in monkery, but to maintain teaching, preaching, study with praying, and good housekeeping [i.e. hospitality]'. For Malvern he made a special plea, commending its prior 'who hath been greatly inclined from the beginning to the

[1] *See* page 111.

virtue of hospitality, and is much commended in these parts for the same. The man is old, feedeth many, and that daily, for the country is poor and full of penury'.

It was of no avail and the priory of Great Malvern was dissolved like other monasteries. Those of its monks who were under twenty-four years of age were absolved from their vows and possibly helped to swell the ranks of sturdy rogues and vagabonds of that period; eight other monks received small allowances; and Richard Whitbourne, the last prior, was granted an annuity of £66 13s. 4d. The monastery buildings were made over to a William Pinnock; he sold them to Sir John Knotsford, whose monument still stands inside the church. His remains must rest uneasily among the scenes of heartless destruction, for all the conventual buildings were pulled down except the Guesten-House, and both the Lady Chapel and south transept were swept away. Mercifully for posterity the villagers of Malvern, headed by a John Pope (who deserves canonization), made an offer for the main church, which they bought for twenty pounds paid in two equal instalments, and so this splendid building was narrowly saved from destruction. This must have been a crumb—a very small crumb—of comfort to those older monks who, although they had been compelled to leave its peaceful walls, yet could not help returning from time to time to gaze in tragic bewilderment upon the ruins of the monastery buildings where they had for so long studied and toiled and prayed.

With the disappearance of the priory and its famous hospitality there was nothing to attract travellers to Malvern, which became once again an obscure village, although by the early seventeenth century its springs had already acquired something of a reputation for their healing properties and, as shown in Chapter III, bottles of Malvern water were being sent all over the country.[1] When in August 1642 Charles the First's standard was unfurled at Nottingham, and the great Civil War began, Malvern had good reason to fear that her countryside would be drawn into the clash of arms. Worcester, the 'Faithful City', was only eight miles away and would surely attract the attention of the contending armies. The worst fears were realized; throughout the war Worcester was a centre of military operations and suffered severely for its

[1] *See* page 31.

devotion to the royal cause. Then, some two years after the execution of his father, when Charles the Second made his desperate bid for the throne, it was to Worcester that he marched with his army from Scotland, and it was at Worcester that he was defeated in the battle which Cromwell described as a 'crowning mercy'.

Parish records of the seventeenth century show how small the village population was, and it is not surprising that their already dilapidated original parish church fell into decay.[1] Indeed they were finding it difficult enough to maintain their newly acquired building, and parish accounts for one year show that the most they could afford to spend on repairs and upkeep in the twelve months was a beggarly twelve pounds. One short but revealing description of the district at this period has been given by that intrepid horsewoman Celia Fiennes, who passed through it when on a visit to a relation and wrote in her *Journal* of the

> Mauborn hills, or as some term them, the English Alps—a Ridge of hills dividing Worcestershire and Herifordshire, and was formerly esteemed the divideing England and Wales. Herriford, Shropshire, etc., were Weltch Countys. They are at least 2 or 3 miles up and are in a Pirramidy fashion on the top. I rode up upon the top of one of the highest, from whence could discern the Country above 40 miles round, and noe hills but what appeared like Burrows or Molehills; these being so high nothing could limmit the eye but distance. On the one side of this high Ridge of hills lies Worcester. Oxford, Glostershire, etc., appears in Plaines, Enclosures, Woods and Rivers, and many great Hills, tho' to this they appear low. On the other side is Herrifordshire which appears like a Country of Gardens and Orchards. The whole Country being very full of fruite trees, etc. it lookes like nothing else, the apple, pear trees, etc., are so thick even in their corn fields and hedgerows. The descent is as long and steep in some places as its rising was.

In the following century another well-known traveller, Daniel Defoe, paid a visit to Malvern, but his account of it in his *Tour Through England and Wales* is perfunctory, inaccurate and obscure:

> Near this city [Worcester] are the famous Malvern Hills, or Mauvern Hills, seen so far every way. In particular, we saw them very plainly on the Downs, between Marlborough

[1] This church of St Thomas stood on the site of the present post office.

and Malmsbury; and they say they are seen from the top of Salisbury steeple which is above 50 miles.

There was a famous monastery at the foot of these hills, on the S.W. side, and the ruins are seen to this day; the old legend of wonders perform'd by the witches of Mauvern, I suppose they mean the religieuse of both kinds, are too merry, as well as too antient for this work.

They talk much of mines of gold and silver, which are certainly to be found here, if they were but look'd for, and that Mauvern wou'd outdo Potosi for wealth; but 'tis probable if there is such wealth, it lies too deep for this idle generation to find out, and perhaps to search for.

Defoe's mention of the supposed 'mines of gold and silver' recalls that the vein of mica, which exists in the ridge between Worcestershire Beacon and the Wyche, has in the past given rise to the idea that there might be a gold-mine beneath the hills, and it is reported that many years ago some eager prospectors even sank a small shaft without, alas, discovering the wealth they had hoped for.

By the end of the eighteenth century the priory church was in a sadly neglected state. Roofs leaked, damp, decay and rot had done their worst, and wanton vandalism had added to the general appearance of ruin inside, where rubbish, broken altar tables and smashed pews littered the floors. One visitor, a well-known architect, was sufficiently shocked to write to the *Gentleman's Magazine*:

I made a survey of this edifice where I am free to declare I was shocked to the utmost sense in beholding so sumptuous a pile, another Westminster Abbey church, though of smaller dimensions, doomed to the worst of defilement and neglect. On the north side of the church was a playground for unrestrained youths whose recreations consisted in throwing stones at the numerous windows, all full of the finest stained glass; and adjoining this playground was a kennel of hounds whose hideous yells filled up at intervals (service time or otherwise) the cry of the headstrong juvenile assailants. In the interior of the church on the north side is a chapel dedicated to our Lord, and called Jesus chapel. Here I actually saw stuck up on its eastern wall a large pigeon house belonging (as my conductor informed me, but to which I could not give any credit) to the parson presiding over the sacred place wherein I then stood, he being equally happy to see the flights of such innocents through the aisles and vaults as to hear the surrounding canine rangers of the sportive fields.

At last the church was described as in 'too ruinous a state to be used with safety', but still nothing appears to have been done to repair it, and in 1805, seven years after its previous report, the *Gentleman's Magazine* published a letter which revealed how much the condition of the building had deteriorated:

> The walls and floors are dreadfully damp, and parts of the church sometimes flooded; the ivy is suffered to grow within the building; at least it has pierced through the interstices formed by the tracery of the eastern window, and covers a large portion of the eastern end of the fabric. It is, in short, in a state unfit for the parishioners, disgraceful to the parish, and will soon be beyond the power of repair.

Even in 1817, in spite of John Wall's early attempts to establish a spa here, Malvern was still only a very small village consisting, according to Chambers, of 'about fifty houses, chiefly neat buildings to which are attached gardens and plantations of fruit, trees, shrubs and evergreens'. It was obviously difficult to raise funds locally for the expensive restoration the church now needed, but in 1809 nearly two thousand pounds was at last obtained and spent on essential repairs to the ceiling, and on cleaning and whitewashing the walls. In the same year the great Malvern 'Brief' was issued in George the Third's name. This was a remarkable document addressed to 'all and singular Archbishops, Bishops, Archdeacons and Deans', and to preachers of all denominations—including Quakers, of all people. The Brief called upon them to ask for and to receive 'Christian and charitable contributions' for the repair of Great Malvern church. In the circumstances it is scarcely surprising that this eccentric appeal collected only £9 19s. od., especially as the Brief also contained a ludicrously vague and unenforceable threat of 'penalties to be inflicted under an Act of the late Queen Anne'.

With the appointment of Henry Card as vicar in 1815 an energetic drive was made to organize a more thorough restoration in stages. After closing the church for some four months it was encouragingly reported that 'the crumbling roof no longer dropped on the uplifted eye of devotion', but some of the new incumbent's disbursements, such as those on building an organ gallery, lining the pews with crimson cloth, and filling a window with the coats of arms of forty-six subscribers to the restoration fund, provoked a certain amount of perhaps not wholly undeserved criticism. A. W. N. Pugin, the pioneer of the revival of Gothic architecture, paid a visit to the church in 1833 and later wrote in a particularly caustic vein:

> I next shaped my course to Malvern to see the Abbey there, and the celebrated Hills. Here is a church in which the stained glass has not fallen a victim to Protestant zeal. It is truly magnificent, and the drawing of the figures is correct and beautiful, the colouring rich and varied. These windows may be rated among the finest specimens of English glass of the fifteenth century. The paving-tiles are likewise decidedly the finest in the kingdom; such a variety of patterns, and such a quantity of tiles I never saw anywhere. A few years ago a meeting of the fashionables of Malvern was called to subscribe towards the repairs of the dilapidated building, and by the help of raffles, etc., a few pounds were collected. Two hodfuls of mortar were got to repair the church, and the remainder of the money expended in putting in a window of the aisle, the arms of the subscribers in stained glass, with their names in full, a monument of their folly and arrogance. The very mullions in which the glass is placed are rotten and falling. The church itself is in dreadful repair; fall it must, and all that is to be hoped is, that in its fall it may annihilate those whose duty it was to have restored it; but of this we may be sure, that if it falls while there is a congregation within its walls it will clear some away that ought to be got rid of, for such a set of lounging idlers as the fashionable of Malvern are only matched at Brighton or Cheltenham.

It was easy enough to criticize and to sneer, but the fact remains that at least Dr Card had roused the apathetic and had taken the first practical steps towards restoring the former glory of his church and making it more worthy of the flourishing town which later developed as a result of the popularity of the Malvern water cure. Indeed, as a later vicar so rightly pointed out,

> in various respects the church of Great Malvern Priory has been singularly fortunate—that it was saved by the

parishioners in 1541, that so large a proportion of its superb glass survived the ages of both violence and neglect, that the decay which would soon have made the building a ruin was checked in the first half of the nineteenth century, and that the 1861–2 'restoration' was, comparatively speaking, conservative in its character.[1]

[1] Canon Anthony C. Deane.

CHAPTER TWO

Royal Forest; Chase; and Conservators

THERE is a common confusion about the meaning of the ancient terms 'forest' and 'chase'. In its original sense a forest was not necessarily a great tract of trees; it was an unenclosed district 'privileged for the abiding of wild beasts and fowls to be under the king's protection for his princely delight and pleasure'. To preserve these hunting rights strictly for the king, the forest (as its ultimate derivation from the Latin *foris*—'outside'—implies) was outside the common law, and special forest courts were set up over which the ordinary courts had no control. When a forest passed out of the sovereign's hands by sale or gift to a subject, it became a chase: 'a place of middle nature between a forest and park, for, properly speaking, a forest cannot be in the hands of a subject, none being able to make a lord chief justice in Eyre but the king'; [1] that is, no one but the king could set up a special jurisdiction over a forest.

The ancient forest of Malvern was in fact thickly wooded—a 'vast wilderness' was William of Malmesbury's description of it —and it was one of the largest of the several forests originally in the county of Worcestershire. Records show that at one period it consisted of over seven thousand acres in Worcestershire, over six hundred acres in Herefordshire and over a hundred acres in Gloucestershire. It contained thirteen parishes, and in some parts was at least twenty miles wide. Even as late as the sixteenth century Leland wrote that 'it is bigger than either Wire or Feckenham Forests, and it occupieth a greate parte of Malvern Hills'; and of course in Leland's time it had shrunk in size and a

---

[1] T. Nash: *Worcestershire.*

good deal of timber was being cut down for building material, for domestic fuel and for the ever increasing needs of the Droitwich salt works where the furnaces were already consuming a prodigious quantity of wood.

The early kings were keen hunters in their forests, even the more serious-minded rulers like Alfred and Edward the Confessor, and the harsh penalties of their forest laws fell with special severity on the poor. Nevertheless the poacher's ancient craft showed no signs of dying out completely. Sometimes from a natural desire to pit their wits against the vigilance of the forest officials, but more often because they were driven by the stark needs of hunger, local peasants continued to snare and even to use the bow in order to replenish their larder.

For some years before the Conquest the holder of Malvern Forest was Brictric Meawe, a trusted Saxon member of the court of Edward the Confessor and Lord of the Manor of Gloucester. He appears to have carried out some kind of diplomatic service for his king which took him to the court of Baldwin, the Count of Flanders. Here, according to one story, he had the misfortune to attract the amorous attentions of the Count's daughter Matilda. To his credit, but unwisely, he refused to respond to feminine advances he felt unable to return, and he was later to learn the bitter truth that

> Heav'n has no rage like love to hatred turn'd,
> Nor Hell a fury like a woman scorn'd.

Matilda succeeded in marrying the Duke of Normandy and thus became the Queen of England when he gained the crown after the battle of Hastings. Her revenge for Brictric's slight was swift and ruthless. The reluctant *eorl* was seized at Hanley Castle and perished miserably in prison at Winchester, and Malvern Forest became another royal forest after it had been given to Matilda herself.

With the accession of William the Conqueror, who 'loved the red deer as if he were their father' and 'took more note of killing a stag than a man', the severity of the forest laws was pushed to barbarous limits. Most of us recall most readily only the picturesque side of the medieval hunt as it is described by contemporary writers like Chaucer, who was himself a deputy forester and shows an intimate knowledge not only of the chase but also of forest woodcraft. It is no mere amateur who wrote the list of trees in *The Parlement of Foules* and described their charactersistics; and the fine description of the hunt in *The Dethe of Blaunche the Duchesse* recaptures all the freshness and vigour of this colourful age. But a poet with courtly connections and holding office as a deputy forester would naturally present the romantic side of hunting and forestry; the grim side seen by ordinary folk in a forest area is sufficiently indicated by the law: 'He who slays a man might be forgiven, not so he who slays a deer. Whosoever killeth a hart is to be blinded.' Originally the punishment for unlawfully killing a deer was indeed death, and barbarous mutilation was prescribed for illegally hunting lesser beasts like the wild boar or wolf. Savage fines were extorted even for killing the humble rabbit or squirrel; and the honey of the wild bees was protected with equal stringency. Permission could sometimes be obtained to feed swine, cattle and horses in the forest at certain fixed periods, but heavy payments were exacted for the privilege. Timber and fuel were also closely guarded, and to despoil the vert by felling trees without the royal licence was an offence punishable by severe penalties.

Malvern Forest was governed by the Lord of Hanley Castle, who had the sole authority under the king of appointing the various forest officers such as the Steward of Hanley and the Chief Forester. He also issued to certain privileged persons the royal grant to hunt and hawk in the forest, but even these grantees were forbidden to exercise their privilege for forty days before and after the king's personal hunting, so that 'the wild beasts might not by any means be disquieted of their rest and peace'. The Chief Forester took a solemn oath to be 'true to the vert and venison', that is to the trees, covert and game, and he appointed various assistants, foresters and woodmen, so that the forest was continually patrolled. All these assistants, and all other persons over twelve years of age who were connected with the forest, were bound under oath 'to be of good behaviour towards his majesty's wild beasts' which was administered in the following words:

Ye shall not hurt do to the beasts of the forest,
Nor to anything that doth belong thereto.
The offence of others ye shall not conceal,
But to the uttermost of your power ye shall them reveal

Unto the officers of the forest,
Or to them that may see the same redressed.
All these things ye shall see done,
So help you God at holie dome.

Those who lived in the forest were permitted to keep a dog only if it had been brought for 'expeditation' to the proper official, the Regarder. Expeditation was effected by striking off three claws of the animal's forepaws with a mallet and chisel, thus making it useless for hunting, and a fee of 'footgeld' was charged for this obligatory operation.

To administer the laws in Malvern Forest the Lord of Hanley Castle held a Court Baron once every three weeks to settle cases of trespass or debt of a minor nature. Those who were accused of unlawful hunting in the forest could be charged under one or more of four offences:

1. *Stable-Stand:* that is, when the prisoner had been caught standing with his bow drawn ready to shoot.
2. *Dog-Draw:* when an animal had been wounded and the prisoner's dog was following or 'drawing' after it.
3. *Back-Bear:* when the accused was caught in the act of carrying the animal away after it had been killed.
4. *Bloody-Hand:* which applied to any prisoner who had been taken in the forest with hands stained by blood.

For more serious cases a Law-Day and Sessions were held, and as the sheriff had no jurisdiction within their territory the forest courts tried even cases of murder and other felonies committed within the forest bounds. A prisoner sentenced to death was taken to a place called Sweet Oak not far from Hanley Castle, and there he was executed with a forester's axe. Then the body was often taken to Baldgate to hang on the hills near the Wyche as a warning to other would-be malefactors; and travellers who made their way across the hills in that direction must often have heard the mournful clank of chains as the grisly remains of unfortunate victims of the forest laws twirled on the gallows in the wind.

Thus for some two hundred years, until the reign of Edward the First, Malvern Forest was the hunting-ground of kings, and no one must have favoured it more than King John, who was a devotee of the chase and who, according to the chronicler

Holinshed, was often 'of right merry humour' and who 'thought it scoffery to pursue any fallow deer with hounds, but tired them out with his own travel on foot'—an unexpectedly light-hearted sidelight on the shifty, vicious monarch who is pictured in school textbooks biting the Runnymede turf in unkingly rage before signing Magna Carta.

When Edward the First's daughter Joan d'Acres married Gilbert de Clare, the eighth Earl of Gloucester, the King presented Malvern Forest to him as part of the wedding dowry, and as a result the name was changed from the royal 'Forest' to 'Malvern Chase' to mark the transfer from king to subject. The proud impetuous Gilbert de Clare was not nicknamed 'the red-headed Earl' for nothing, and all too soon he was involved in a violent quarrel with the Bishop of Hereford over their respective hunting territories. The Bishop was in the habit of hunting over the land west of the hills which he asserted was his right, and he used his country house at Colwall as a hunting-lodge for this purpose. The fiery Earl hotly contested the Bishop's claims, but his threats had no effect on the cool determination of this ecclesiastic to continue his hunting. Finally a suit-at-law was begun to decide who was right in this quarrel. It seems that the judges appointed to investigate the dispute decided that the Bishop's claim should be allowed. The baffled Earl continued to see game he was pursuing take refuge on the Bishop's territory west of the hills, and then fall a prey to his episcopal rival. In retaliation he constructed a ditch along the boundary, or more probably reconstructed an ancient earthwork which already existed there. To make the passage of deer even more difficult he also set up a palisade of sharp stakes along its length, and he swore that any Bishop's men who crossed this boundary would not even live to regret it. The Red Earl's Dyke is marked on modern maps and can still be traced on the summit of the hills. After this legal clash, feelings ran so high that, according to one story, a supporter of the Bishop issued a challenge to the Red Earl, the Bishop himself being of course debarred from doing so by virtue of his peaceful calling. Joan, the Red Earl's wife, now peremptorily took control of the quarrel, and she persuaded the King to forbid the duel on the grounds that her husband (who was some fifty years of age) was well past the age of risking his life in such dangerous, youthful escapades.

The succession of owners of Malvern Chase during the next two hundred years is complicated and need not be traced here, but the Chase came into possession of Richard, Earl of Warwick, the 'King-maker', through his wife Anne Beauchamp who was a lineal descendant of the Red Earl. Some twenty years after Warwick's death at the battle of Barnet, Henry the Seventh took possession of Malvern Chase which, technically at least, once more became a forest, but it was no longer the place it once had been. Hanley Castle was first neglected, then deserted, and finally lay in ruins. Poachers had been making free with the game; the fine timber began to disappear; and squatters spread over the once closely guarded hunting-ground. The forest was further dismembered when Henry the Eighth gave away a large tract of it, and when later Queen Elizabeth the First presented portions of it to her chancellor and various other people.

Charles the First's continual pressing need for money made him decide to sell what remained of the once extensive royal forest, but by now commoners and squatters were firmly settled, and they were determined to retain what they had won for themselves. The King's decision to sell was a threat to their recently won rights, and they expressed their disapproval by riots. After many ugly disturbances the King finally agreed on a compromise: he gave up two-thirds of the territory in question to the commoners, but retained the remaining one-third. The final disafforesting decree was promulgated in 1632 ordering that 'none of the forest should be enclosed except His Majesty's one-third, and that the other two-thirds should be left open and free for the freeholders and tenants and commoners to take their common of pasture as heretofore they have been accustomed'.

The King's share was purchased by his Attorney-General, Sir R. Heath, and by Sir Cornelius Vermuyden. The latter lived on uneasy terms with the commoners, who often complained bitterly that he was exceeding his legal rights in the old forest territory, while he continually accused them of preventing his enjoyment of the rights he had paid for when he bought the property from the King. The land which the commoners thus obtained included much valuable common land which we can enjoy today—Link Common, Malvern Common, Wells Common, Castlemorton Common, Bernard's Green and Sherrard's Green.

Towards the end of the nineteenth century increasing encroachments on the hills and enclosures of portions of the commons threatened to destroy the unique characteristics of this beautiful and historic territory. Indiscriminate building and, above all, the ever increasing quarrying activities presented problems which could only be dealt with by the authorized measures of a legally constituted body. Fortunately the dangers were faced just in time, and in 1884 the Malvern Hills Act was passed to prevent further enclosures and encroachments. It set up a Board of 'Conservators' with statutory powers and duties to preserve the natural beauties of the hills and commons. The members of the Board are partly elected and partly nominated by certain local authorities which are affected by the rate which the Conservators have the power to levy. This was the first of several Acts passed at various times between 1884 and 1930 which give the Conservators the authority not only to precept a rate for expenses but also to make and enforce by-laws, to construct and maintain roads and paths, to plant trees, to appoint keepers and to acquire additional land. To check further depredations by quarrying they have also acquired various mineral rights which otherwise would have been exercised to the further detriment of the hills, especially on the skyline. In 1935 the efforts of the Conservators were considerably encouraged when over a thousand acres at the southern end of the hills were acquired by the National Trust with the help of the Pilgrim Trust and the public-spirited co-operation of several landowners. The ever growing volume of motor traffic, above all at week-ends, continues to present serious problems, but so far the Conservators have managed to provide sufficient parking spaces without sacrificing too much of the natural beauty at the foot of the hills.

Occasionally there are criticisms, not always well informed, of some of the activities of the Conservators and of their regulations, but it is impossible to deny that without their vigilance and energetic administration, the Malvern Hills and commons would hardly exist in their present state but, like so many other ravished areas of natural beauty, would have been built over, driven over and generally desecrated by the ruthless march of modern progress.

CHAPTER THREE

Taking the Malvern Waters

MALVERN became a popular spa at a comparatively late period in its history but its various wells were known from earliest times. In his *History of Malvern* John Chambers claims that the oldest of the Malvern wells was 'a spring called Ditchford's Well or Mary's and Nancy's Well, which names have been presumed to be belonging to the women who carried the water of this spring in bottles, on horseback, to Worcester'. More famous, however, were the Holy Well above Malvern Wells, and St Ann's Well at Great Malvern. Both wells rise on the eastern side of the hills which would impart an added virtue to the water, for 'waters that are exposed to the rising of the sun must needs be clear, of a good smell, soft and pleasant; for the sun by rising and shining upon them prevents any bad effects from the damp of the morning, which the air diffuses for the most part everywhere'.

To be a 'holy' well, and to bear the name of a saint, suggests that both these two springs were venerated from an early period, possibly even in a pre-Christian era, for as Dom Ethelbert Horne has pointed out,

in course of time when the Christian missionary came upon the scene, he preached and taught at places where men had gathered—that is, round these springs of water. Then the converts would need baptism, and so the well was made use of for the purpose, and probably its old heathen dedication was changed into a Christian one from that day onwards. We know how careful the new teachers were not to wound the feelings of these pagans by making too sudden a break with the past, and so just as they re-dedicated their temples and re-named their feast days, they put their wells under the protection of some saint in place of the pagan deity who had previously presided over them. As the ages went on, the

29

memory of the holy man who had taught Christianity on any given spot was treasured up, and the well where he had given the sacrament of baptism was looked upon as something sacred. When sickness came these waters were used with faith and were said to have a healing virtue through the intercession of the saint now long with God.

The use of Malvern waters for curative purposes is mentioned as long ago as the early seventeenth century, when in Richard Banister's *Breviary of the Eye* they are described as especially efficacious in cases of eye troubles:

> A little more I'll of their curing tell,
> How they help sore eyes with a new-found well;
> Great speech of Malvern Hills was lately reported,
> Unto which spring people in troops resorted.

It is remarkable that the water of almost all holy wells throughout the country was regarded as a panacea for diseases of the eye. This, Ethelbert Horne suggests, can also be traced back to a religious origin:

> Here and there a spring has a reputation for curing skin complaints or sprains, but it would be probably true to say that ninety-five out of every hundred yield water that is 'good for the eyes'. Why the eyes? No satisfactory answer can be given to the question, although many more or less probable solutions have been suggested. Perhaps the one that has most to be said in its favour is that as the majority of these springs owed their title of 'holy' to the fact that it was in them the first missionaries gave the sacrament of baptism, so it was by these waters that the recipient came out of the blindness of heathenism into the light of faith. This spiritual sight which baptism was said to give to the soul was taken, as time went on, to mean sight to the eyes, and hence rose the common belief in the efficacy of the water from these wells for all complaints which affected the seeing.

Another seventeenth-century poem written in praise of Malvern makes special mention of its healing waters:

> Out of that famous hill
>   There daily springeth
> A water, passing still,
>   Which always bringeth

Great comfort to all them
That are diseased men,
And makes them well again,
   To praise the Lord.

Hast thou a wound to heal,
 The which doth grieve thee?
Come then unto this well,
 It will relieve thee;
Noli me tangeres,
And other maladies,
Have here their remedies,
   Prais'd be the Lord.

To drink thy water's store,
 Lie in thy bushes
Many with ulcers sore,
 Many with bruises;
Who succour find from ill,
By money given still,
Thanks to the Christian will:
   O praise the Lord.

A thousand bottles there
 Were filled weekly,
And many costrils rare,
 For stomachs sickly;
Some of them into Kent,
Some were to London sent,
Others to Berwick went,
   O praise the Lord.

It is interesting to read that even at this early date Malvern water was being bottled and sent to such distant places in the country. Its fame was certainly known to John Evelyn, who visited the hills about this time and recorded in his Diary:

August 1, 1654: We set out towards Worcester and by the way (thick planted with Cider fruit) we deviate to the holy Wells trickling out of a Vally, thro a steepe declivity towards the foote of Greate-Maubern hills. They are said to heale many infirmities, as Kings-Evil, Leaprosie, etc., sore eyes. Ascending a greate height above them to the trench dividing England from South Wales we had the prospect of all

Herefordshire, Radnor, Brecknock, Monmouth, Worcester, Gloucester, Shropshire, Warwick, Derbyshire, and many more. We could discern Tewxbery, Kingsrode towards Bristol, etc., and so I esteeme it one of the goodliest vistas in England.

The first move to establish Malvern as a spa on a commercial basis was made by that remarkable Worcester worthy Dr Wall. John Wall is a good example of the versatile eighteenth-century Englishman of parts. The son of a well-to-do Worcester trades- man who became mayor of the city, he was educated at the local grammar school and at Oxford, where he qualified in medicine. He was not only a physician of high repute, but also an artist of no mean ability. To posterity he is perhaps best known as the founder of the world-famous Worcester porcelain works, but in Malvern he is best remembered as the first doctor to make scientific claims for the medicinal virtues of Malvern waters. He planned his campaign with typical shrewdness, and began by publishing a short treatise on the remarkable cures effected by the water at Malvern in the past. These included cases of palsy, scrofula, ulcers and the restoration of failing sight. One old lady is reported to have recovered sufficiently from her blindness to have the doubtful advantage of being able once again to see the fleas hopping over her bedclothes.

Among the greatest attractions of some of the most popular and most remunerative spas in this country and abroad was the unpleasant taste of their waters, which was considered a sure proof of their virtue. Malvern water, on the other hand, is unusually pleasant to drink and has a sparkling brightness which suggests absolute purity unadulterated by any curative sub- stances, but John Wall was determined to find some. He subjected the water to the most stringent tests then available. These revealed that the water was indeed of almost unparalleled purity, 'only pure element, devoid of mineral spirit and of almost all other principles'—a discovery which provoked the local jest:

> The Malvern water, says Dr John Wall,
> Is famed for containing just nothing at all!

Dr Wall was unperturbed; and determined to make a virtue of necessity he stressed that the value of Malvern water lay in the very fact of its freedom from the disagreeable, malodorous characteristics of most other spa water. For 'the efficacy of this water seems chiefly to arise from its great purity, whereby it passes through the smallest vessels, and not being loaded with any salts or earth it is capable of dissolving more than those waters which are already saturated with them. Its effects externally, both in lotion and bathing, may in a great measure depend upon the same, since it is past all doubt that fluids may enter the body in this way by the absorbing vessels'.

Dr Wall had made his point with some success; he had substituted an impressive scientific jargon for the former faith in a cure by miraculous means and this, coupled with three editions of his book, encouraged the growth of Malvern as a spa. He attracted a number of fashionable patients to Malvern Wells, many of them typical topers and gluttons of the period who could scarcely fail to benefit from a regimen of pure water, fresh air and regular exercise in such healthy surroundings.

During the eighteen years he practised at Malvern, John Wall's pioneering efforts began to transform the village into a popular health resort. There were the usual assembly balls and, a year after Dr Wall's arrival, John Dugard's Lodging House and Assembly Room were advertising 'public breakfasts for one shilling and sixpence, and afterwards the Shepherd Lottery will be played. N.B. Musicians will be in waiting in order to perform if the company should be disposed for a dance'—an outstanding example of the vigour of our ancestors that even companies of invalids taking a cure could indulge in such hearty exercise during what a softer generation has come to regard as the silent meal of the day.

After John Wall's retirement to Bath in 1774 the number of visitors fell off for a time, but soon revived sufficiently to encourage the building of a number of hotels to supplement the lodgings which had up to then provided most of the accommodation. The Foley Arms first catered for visitors about 1810, and in time was so well patronized that it was considerably enlarged. The Bellevue Hotel also became a well-known hostelry, and although it has now been transformed into a row of shops, the word 'Hotel' is still faintly visible beside 'Bellevue' on the wall. In Malvern Wells, the present Wells House Preparatory School was at a later period a select lodging-house kept by a Mr Steers. The Holy Well was presided over by elderly women 'with cheerful faces and in clean white aprons'. They were also responsible for keeping the paths tidy around the well, and in the large dining-room of Mr Steers's lodging-house there was a card with the 'humble inscription of Ann Farmer who at the age of seventy sweeps the walks near the Wells House, relying for support on the visitors to Malvern', and inevitably breaking into doggerel verse:

> This humble petition I beg leave to show,
> For sweeping the walks above and below,
> From the top of the hills down to the Well House,
> There is not a stone so large as a mouse.

An additional fillip was given to the growing spa at Malvern by the visit of the young Princess Victoria, who, with her mother, the Duchess of Kent, stayed at Holly Mount and regularly rode up to the hills on a donkey which was christened 'Royal Moses' in her honour. Donkeys were for many years the favoured means of conveyance for the elderly or the less energetic up to St Ann's Well, or the foothills of the Malverns. They plied for hire in dozens near the hotels, and a nineteenth-century guide reassuringly remarked that 'the donkeys are useful appendages in ascending the hills, being very sure-footed; indeed they are so perfectly safe that in twelve years we do not recollect one accident occasioned by a donkey'.

The same guide-book put in a special plea for donkeys and their drivers, and for cabmen:

> The donkeys and horses of our watering-places are often a hardly used and much abused race, and generally the fault lies in those who use them, and not in those to whose care they are committed. The party who engages an animal has it in his power to prevent an undue strain on its energies, as well as the improper application of the whip. Donkey drivers are not infrequently made impudent or presuming by undue familiarity, or by being converted into objects of merriment and joke. A benevolent and kindhearted visitor may induce a healthy influence on the youthful mind by a healthy tone of conversation. . . . Every ride or drive may quietly be converted into the exercise of a moral gift, and without the appearance of intrusion or cant.
>
> The cabman who works hard during six days of the week ought, with the horse he tends, even on mere physical

grounds to enjoy a rest on one day in the seven. Many cab-men complain that, through being compelled to convey others to public worship, they are prevented from taking part in it themselves. A little timely arrangement or con-siderate self-denial on the part of visitors and invalids would largely tend to benefit a hard-working and deserving class of men.

Visitors to Malvern were often pestered by beggars and were warned not to encourage them by giving alms indiscriminately. They were mostly impostors ready with a plausible story for any listener benevolent and gullible enough to believe it and to give them charity which was generally liquidated in the local ale-house. Some of the tricksters were only too well known to local residents who saw them return summer after summer to impor-tune the unwary visitor. One was a Mrs Moloney, who openly boasted that she came 'every sayson' to beg at Malvern, and her blarney seemed to keep her in comparative comfort for the rest of the year. Another regular character was a girl who could turn on her tears to order at the sight of a rich kindly old gentleman, and would sob bitterly saying she had just lost her only shilling.

It seems strange that Malvern had to wait until the middle of the nineteenth century before the real commercial possibilities of its water cure were properly exploited. It was in May of 1842 that Dr James Wilson and Dr James Manby Gully arrived at the Crown Hotel [1] and decided that Malvern was indeed (to use the ominous modern phrase) 'ripe for development' as a spa. Dr Wilson had been at Graefenberg as a patient and pupil under Vincenz Priessnitz, the pioneer of 'hydropathy', which pro-claimed that 'water is the supreme general cure for disease'. Used internally and externally it could overcome 'the evils of a stomach generally overworked, and a skin under-worked'. To correct former excesses, patients were also made to take exercise until they were ravenous, but still 'hunger reigned supreme at Graefenberg'.

Dr Wilson returned to England fired with these new ideas and determined to set up a similar water spa in this country. Malvern was chosen as the most suitable place, and Wilson took over the lease of the Crown Hotel, renamed it Graefenberg House and began his hydropathic practice. Shortly afterwards, Gully joined

[1] Its site is now occupied by Lloyd's Bank.

him and built his own establishments, Tudor House for men and
Holyrood House for women, joined together by what the male
patients irreverently dubbed 'The Bridge of Sighs'.[1]

Both doctors soon attracted a large and lucrative practice,
although the Malvern water cure was unusually strict and made
few concessions to the frailties of the flesh. It combined an in-
ordinate consumption of the water with a remorseless series of
'hydropathic processes' which were capable of various combinations and modifications. For example, after the regulation call at
5 a.m. the patient might be ordered the 'Pack', and then the whole
of his body was enveloped in sheets wrung out of cold or tepid
water while 'all evaporation is prevented by the sheets being
adequately enveloped in blankets'. At some stage in Dr Gully's
establishment a patient was allowed the apparent luxury of the
'Lamp Bath'. He sat wrapped in blankets on a chair under which
a lamp was burning. This was claimed to be 'an admirable
sudorific inducing speedy free action of the skin with the advantage over the Turkish Bath that the patient inhales the natural air,
and is not necessarily compelled to breathe a highly heated
atmosphere'. One nervous patient once asked the attendant if
anyone had ever been burnt by this treatment. 'Yes,' came the
laconic reply, 'but not yet in this establishment.' In any case, the
lamp bather was not allowed to enjoy the comfort of his warmth
for long; the treatment was immediately followed by the 'Shallow
Bath' of cold water, 'the force or shock with which the water is
dashed upon the body varying with each patient, and also the
time of immersion'.

In case the patient was not already sufficiently cowed there was
also the 'Sitz Bath', in which he was made to sit 'at various
depths, different temperatures, and for different periods of time
according to the medical end required, whether tonic and bracing,
or derivative and cooling'—no end was ever 'comforting'.

Finally, as an exquisite refinement of torture, patients could be
prescribed the 'Douche'. It is always surprising to know what the
human body can put up with, but it certainly was a test of
endurance to stand naked for as long as one and a half minutes
beneath a pipe while it discharged more than fifty gallons of ice-
cold water, even with the comforting knowledge that it had been

[1] Together they now form the Tudor Hotel.

recommended as 'a powerful water agency, useful in cases where it is a suitable remedy, but a process which demands special care in its adaptation'.

One patient left a vivid written description of his feelings when he was given this treatment for the first time. 'When it struck me straight on the shoulder it knocked me clean over like a ninepin. A momentary rush, like a thunderstorm, was heard over me, and the next second the water came roaring through the pipe like a lion upon its prey and struck me on the shoulders with a merciless bang, spinning me about like a teetotum.' The ritual observed to call each patient was in itself sufficient to increase the understandable anxieties of those who were waiting their turn. The door would open, an attendant motioned without speaking, and the victim disappeared into the 'Douche' hut where there was silence until the sudden splashing rush of water accompanied by hoarse exclamations from a male patient, or half-scared, half-rapturous shrieks from a female sufferer. Nor were the stories with which the attendant regaled the patients calculated to inspire confidence. One was of a patient who during a cold season was momentarily stunned by a large icicle which fell from the pipe. Another told of a stout lady who mounted a chair in order to shorten the fall of the water, but whose weight, increased by the force of the torrent, caused the collapse of the chair.

The Malvern spa was also introduced to the very latest kind of treatment by Dr E. B. Grindrod, who at his establishment was one of the first in this country to use the 'Compressed Air Chamber' therapy. Although these strange air-tight iron rooms were already in use in France, 'the one in Malvern is the largest ever constructed, being adequate to a *séance* of ten or twelve individuals. It is built of strong iron plates capable of resisting several times the pressure to which it is subjected, with adequate light and several windows of extremely thick glass. The room is hung with pictures, and invalids can recline on sofas or easy chairs, and can engage in unexciting games or occupy themselves in reading, painting, and other light amusements. It is an invaluable treatment in complaints of the respiratory organs; and in croup the compressed air will flatten down the adventitious membranes. In disorders arising from weakness, the compressed air will arterialize the blood and increase the vital power of the patient'. To give additional confidence to those who were subjected to this increased atmospheric pressure Grindrod himself could be seen through a small glass window, seated in the control room, watching his patients' reactions with the keenest interest.

The water-drinking part of the cure was combined with healthy exercise. The patient was armed with a Graefenberg flask —'a sort of tumbler flattened as though you had put it in your pocket soft, and then sat on it'—and then set off to climb the hill-side to St Ann's Well. After consuming his draught there he proceeded to walk to various other springs, drinking his fill at each until he had completed the prescribed tour. Charles Dickens, who was at Malvern in 1851, wrote to John Forster:

> It is a most beautiful place, but O heaven, to meet the Cold Waterers (as I did this morning when I went out for a shower-bath) dashing down the hills, with severe expressions on their countenances, like men doing matches and not exactly winning! Then, a young lady in a grey polka going *up* the hills, regardless of legs; and meeting a young gentle-man (a bad case, I should say) with a light black silk cap on under his hat, and the pimples of I don't know how many douches under that. Likewise an old man who ran over a milk-child rather than stop!—with no neckcloth, on principle; and with his mouth wide open to catch the morning air.

It is only fair to add that Dr Wilson at least took his own medicine, and it is recorded that on one occasion he consumed thirty flasks of water before breakfast, claiming that it made him cheerful, hungry and alert. 'You wash your face with water,' he would say heartily, 'so why not your stomach, too?'

Macaulay was at Malvern in the same year as Dickens, but he seemed much less occupied with the water cure than with the vagaries of the conveyances which plied in the district. He spent the months of August and September in a pleasant villa 'em-bowered in a wood full of blackbirds', and invited his friend the lawyer Thomas Ellis to join him.

Malvern: August 21, 1851.

Dear Ellis,

I shall expect you on Wednesday next. I have got the tickets for the Messiah. There may be some difficulty about conveyances during the festival. But the supply here is immense. On every road round Malvern coaches and flys pass you every ten minutes, to say nothing of irregular vehicles. For example, the other day I was overtaken by a hearse as I was strolling along. 'Would you like a ride, Sir?' said the driver. 'Plenty of room.' I could not help laughing. 'I dare say I shall want such a carriage some day or other. But I am not ready yet.' The fellow, with the most consummate gravity, answered, 'I meant, Sir, that there was plenty of room on the box.'

I am planning various excursions. We can easily see Hereford between breakfast and dinner one day, and Gloucester on another. Cheltenham, and Tewkesbury with its fine church, are still more accessible.

Ever yours,

T. B. MACAULAY.

The most amusing account of the Malvern water cure was published anonymously in 1858 with the title *Three Weeks in Wet Sheets: Being the Diary and Doings of a Moist Visitor to Malvern*. It was the work of Joseph Leech, a Bristol journalist whose genial writings enlivened the *Bristol Times and Mirror*, of which he was part proprietor. Leech decided to go to Malvern because, as he put it, 'I felt I required rest, and I fancied I wanted abstinence, and the best place to have both, with the two great elements of air and water in proportion, was in some of those hydropathic houses which stand at the base of the Malvern Hills.' The 'Moist Visitor' faithfully records the details of his three weeks' visit with shrewd observation and delightful humour. When he made his first round of the springs with his Graefenberg flask he found that a crowd had already gathered at the well, and they were 'all at work filling themselves like so many water casks. One of the company had a tin saucepan with a long handle with which he baled from the well into the glasses of the water drinkers. They drank slowly, sipped or sucked in the element as though it were '20 port and they wished to make every delicious drop of it touch the palate before passing down'.

At the next well he found a similar group who were 'at work imbibing as earnestly as ever with the same nose-in-glass and glassy stare as before. I thought of what old Weller said of the guests at the tea party: "They were a wisibly swellin' afore my eyes, sir."' Leech continued on his way, and arrived at yet another spring to find the familiar faces of some of the same patients, 'and by this time', he wrote, 'they had, I suspect, swallowed enough, if well shaken, to make them rattle like so many Spanish water skins or milk pail panniers'.

The doctors—Wilson in particular—ruled the patients with a rod of iron, especially on the question of diet. Generals and admirals whose very voices would have struck terror into their subordinates were 'as deferential to the water doctors as any drummer-boy or middy'. Barristers whose lashing tongues were famous in cross-examination cringed to them, their spirit broken by the 'Douche'. If rules were disobeyed, they were disobeyed in secret. On his arrival at Great Malvern the 'Moist Visitor' had found in the hotel bar 'a water patient who had obviously broken bounds at nightfall and gratified his thirst by ordering in guilty tones a glass of brandy and water. Swallowing it hastily he then took to flight'. Smoking was strictly forbidden by Dr Wilson and, like many others patients, Leech fell from grace by climbing up the hills between the Worcestershire Beacon and Sugar Loaf Hill, where he smoked a delicious cigar with 'that guilty dread and excitement that Guy Fawkes would have had if he had got near to firing Parliament'; and all the while he found himself looking around surreptitiously to make sure that Dr Wilson himself was not in sight.

The 'Moist Visitor' was courageous enough to complete his three weeks at Malvern, and finally departed 'delighted on the whole with my stay but longing again for a life of a little more care, and from my pastoral retreat I sighed for even the excitement of a bad debt'. He was so well satisfied with the treatment that he promised Dr Wilson he would send up the whole bench of Bristol aldermen to be washed out.

'"Do," said the doctor. "And send the mayor, too." I shook my head; but should His Worship or the Worshipful bench be disposed to try the water treatment they have my personal assurance of the purity of the element.'

The novelist Lord Lytton wrote ecstatically of the water cure:

As health depends upon healthful habits, let those who desire easily and luxuriously to glide into the courses most agreeable to the human frame, to enjoy the morning breeze, to grow epicures in the simple regimen, to become cased in armour against the vicissitudes of our changeful skies—to feel, and to shake off light sleep as a blessed dew, let them, while their organs are yet sound and their nerves yet un-shattered, devote an autumn to the water cure.

But even he was tempted by hunger (and by Eve in the shape of some lady friends) to creep into a Malvern pastry-cook's and buy a dozen rich tarts. Alas, on coming out he was confronted by the redoubtable Dr Wilson himself.

'What have you been buying in there, sir?'

Lytton meekly showed his purchase.

'Poison!' shouted the doctor. 'Throw them away at once, sir!'

Taking one last longing look at the forbidden fruit Lytton obediently dropped them into the gutter.

As the number of visitors grew, local trade increased, and the guide-books provided a useful medium for advertisers. Some of these mid nineteenth-century advertisements make amusing and interesting reading today, especially when contemporary prices are mentioned. For example, a well-recommended hotel at Malvern Link offered 'single beds at one shilling and sixpence to three shillings per day, with two shillings to four shillings extra for a private sitting-room. Attendance is an extra one shilling per day. Families and gentlemen boarded by the week at two pounds ten shillings each person, including attendance'. Another announcement welcomed the 'reduction of duty on tea from one shilling to sixpence per pound which will prove a great blessing to all lovers of the beverage', and offered 'Congou Tea, 1/6d. a pound; useful Congou Tea, 2/– a pound; and very superior, rich and strong Congou, 3/– a pound'.

The doctors were inevitably followed by the dentists, and Mr Rogers, surgeon dentist, claimed that his

> improvements in replacing ARTIFICIAL TEETH have entirely superseded those constructed on the ordinary principles, in appearance, utility, durability and economy. They are guaranteed never to change colour, being fixed without wires on the only correct principle, that of being useful to the wearer. No painful operation is required, ensuring most perfect articulation, and comfort in mastication.

Rather more on the fringe of Malvern's medical activities was 'MESMERISM, GALVANISM AND RUBBING'.

> Mr. J. Swinton, late of Edinburgh, attends patients requiring advice and treatment as above either at his own residence,

Saint Ann's Cottage, Church Street, Malvern, or at the residence of his patients. Mr. Swinton has successfully treated nervous diseases of all kinds—palsy, rheumatism, sciatica, bodily deformities, etc., etc., and will have much pleasure in submitting for inspection numerous testimonials of the highest order from medical men and others.

Nor was the persistent struggle to preserve the youthful appearance neglected, and BEETHAM'S HAIR FLUID was advertised as an infallible hair restorer and preventative of greyness:

It is used by the Royal Family, Ladies and Gentlemen of the Court of Her Majesty, and thousands of the Aristocracy and Gentry. All attempts to imitate it during the last fifteen years have failed. It strengthens and promotes the growth of fine and weak hair; effectually prevents falling out; and possesses the wonderful properties of restoring its colour when turning grey without the use of dyes. In India its effects have been marvellous in restoring the hair of baldness. The beautiful gloss it imparts is truly enchanting. Bottles 2/6d. to 7/6d.

Striking a more sombre note Edward Gwynn advertised himself as 'a Joiner and Coffin-Maker' who was always ready to undertake 'jobbing of every description, including the supply of cornice poles and venetian blinds'. Another firm made a speciality of supplying families with 'deep or complimentary mourning outfits'. Their main stock consisted splendidly enough of 'Italian Cords; Venetian Cords; Barathea Figure; Dye-warp Paramattas; Silk-warp Henrietta; Twill Coburg Cloth; and Alpaca Lustre', but with ill-concealed pride, one feels, they then listed their more exotic materials which have names ringing out like the rich tones of organ chords: 'French Merinos; Gotha Cloths; French Delaines; Cashmeres and Mohairs; Paris Pin Cords; Tamataves and Bareges; Grenadines, Crystallines, Challes and Ariels.'

Before long other doctors settled in Malvern, dazzled by the success of Wilson, Gully and Grindrod. Among them were Dr Paisley, who practised at West Malvern; Edward Johnson, who set up at 'Malvernbury' and 'Ellerslie'; Dr Ayerst, who built 'Wells House'; and J. L. Marsden, who joined Dr Gully in his practice. Some of the newcomers, like Marsden, a homoeopath, as well as the original three, antagonized the more orthodox general practitioners, who would otherwise have accepted their treatment as a useful adjunct to more conventional medicine. One big gun, Sir Charles Hastings, the founder of the British Medical Association, had retired to Malvern, and he fired at them through the powerful columns of the *British Medical Journal*.

Echoes of these attacks may well have been heard by the general public, but there were other reasons why Malvern Spa lost its popularity almost as rapidly as it had gained it. Charges there had always been high, almost excessive—at one period Gully was said to be earning over ten thousand pounds a year, an enormous income in those days. For these fees patients submitted to an almost intolerably meagre diet and Spartan discipline. Now that more settled conditions and better travelling facilities on the Continent made it easier to travel abroad, wealthy patrons preferred to go to foreign spas, which offered a more benign regimen and social attractions like gambling which transformed the 'cure' into a 'holiday'.

It must also be remembered that the original Malvern water cure had been created by dynamic 'characters' like Wilson, Gully and Grindrod. Their spa had certainly had its share of fame and success during their heyday, and their patients had included famous figures like Gladstone, Dickens, Carlyle, Tennyson, Darwin and Florence Nightingale, to mention only a few; but Wilson died in 1867, Gully left Malvern five years later, and the last of the trio, Grindrod, died a few years afterwards. With their departure the spa too soon disappeared with one of those sudden ebbs of history. Some hydropathic establishments became hotels or schools, but Malvern had also to turn elsewhere to seek other sources of prosperity.

CHAPTER FOUR

Elgar and Shaw in Malvern

EDWARD ELGAR, our greatest composer since Purcell, was born within sight of the Malvern Hills, and his affection for them throughout his life suggests how much they had influenced his sensitive imagination as a child. In boyhood he had eagerly absorbed every scrap of history and legend associated with the countryside around his birthplace, and in old age, as W. H. Reed recalls, he loved nothing better than to be driven through the lanes and byways he knew so well—to the small cottage at Birchwood where he had scored *The Dream of Gerontius*, and to Longdon Marsh where in the solitude of those mysterious willow-lined flats he had found inspiration for a great deal of *The Apostles*.

Leaving school at the age of fourteen, Elgar had a very brief spell in a solicitor's office, and then, by his own choice, began the struggling life of a provincial professional musician. He helped in his father's music shop at Worcester; he became his assistant organist at St George's Roman Catholic church; and he played the violin in local amateur orchestras and at the Three Choirs Festival. He became the conductor of a local glee club and of the band at the Worcester County Lunatic Asylum; and he composed and scored a great deal of music for an extraordinary variety of unusual combinations of instruments. In addition to all this he built up a teaching practice, and Malvern, the flourishing spa with its select girls' schools, provided admirable opportunities for a professional musician who had by now acquired something of a reputation locally and who was moreover a personable young man, yet at the same time 'of quiet studious habits' and thus eminently suitable for teaching impressionable young ladies. Elgar has been described as somewhat shy and diffident at this period, and there was some surprise when at the age of thirty-two he married one of his pupils, Alice Roberts, the daughter of a distinguished major-general.[1]

Immediately after their marriage, in order to justify his wife's profound faith in his genius, Elgar gave up his professional engagements in Malvern and the neighbourhood, and they moved to London where it was hoped that his abilities would have wider and more lucrative recognition. After two years of unrewarded struggle, and fruitless rounds of music publishers, a bitterly disillusioned Elgar was writing to various people for permission to use their names as references so that he could once again build up his former teaching connections. On 20th June 1891 they returned to Malvern and moved into a small house which they named 'Forli' after the fifteenth-century Italian artist whose paintings of angels playing musical instruments had always been special favourites of theirs. They were to remain in Malvern for the next thirteen years, and it was here that Elgar's ambitious hopes began at last to be realized, and where some of his finest earlier work was written.

After an initial period of illness and depression Elgar was soon involved in a round of activities which, even if they did not produce much of an income, at least brought him friends and kept him busy, and his creative powers alive, in surroundings which he and his wife loved. He continued to teach a considerable number of pupils, a not wholly congenial task; 'like turning a grindstone with a dislocated shoulder', was his description of it. He also took his place again as violinist in local orchestral performances, and wrote works which showed ever increasing technical ability and gradually earned for him a reputation much wider than that of 'the young Malvern composer'.

'Forli', a semi-detached house in Alexandra Road,[2] had a small lawn and a tennis court in front shared by the occupants of both the attached houses. Behind it the North Hill rises up stark and sheer, showing the gashes of its quarrying. Today the house seems somewhat hemmed in and hardly suggests R. J. Buckley's description of it as 'a charming cottage, meet situation for the dreamy tone-poet, the creator of ravishing harmonies'. Buckley visited the composer about three years after his return to Malvern. His cantata *The Black Knight* had already been produced at

---

[1] *See page* 119.
[2] The house now bears a plaque recording Elgar's residence there.

Worcester, and he was now engaged on the task of correcting the proofs of his first oratorio, *The Light of Life*. Buckley found him working in a small bell tent which had been pitched on the lawn. Above the tent pole fluttered a flag indicating, half in jest and half in earnest, that the composer was busy and was not to be disturbed. Inside were easy chairs, a table and a couch; and scattered about were sheets of music paper scrawled over with Elgar's spidery notation and his special private hieroglyphics. His visitor had the impression of a man who was resolved 'to make the world aware of the power he believed to be his own'.

A friend who has left a more intimate study of the Elgars at 'Forli' was Mrs Richard Powell, the 'Dorabella' of the *Enigma Variations*. She confirms that Elgar preferred to work whenever possible in his tent on the lawn, however stuffy it might be. For relaxation he loved to walk on the hills, pointing out various landmarks to his visitors and relating all kinds of historical events connected with the district. An inveterate leg-puller, he would sometimes tease his more gullible listeners by inventing remarkable 'facts' about the Malvern countryside. The Elgars were avid readers; their rooms were crammed with books, and they were among the first members of a Malvern book club formed to enable members to exchange books from one another's libraries.

Although he was much overworked and still a relatively poor man, these Malvern years were perhaps the happiest of Elgar's life. He had a devoted wife, a small daughter Carice, a number of close friends, and several absorbing hobbies which he pursued with characteristic zest. Besides his walking and cycling, he played golf and billiards with erratic but enthusiastic vigour, and he was a passionate devotee of the current craze of kite-flying, which he could indulge in to his heart's content on the hills. Over the sitting-room fireplace at 'Forli' a board was embellished with poker work representing the flashing semiquavers of one of the 'Fire Motifs' from Wagner's *Ring*, a product of one of his indoor hobbies which later included rough and ready carpentry and chemistry.

After *The Black Knight* came another cantata, *King Olaf*, which was performed at Hanley and also in London; but his next work, dedicated to the Queen, was directly inspired by the Malvern Hills, and its subject was suggested by his mother when she was staying at Colwall. They had been standing together watching the evening sunlight on the Herefordshire Beacon. 'Look at that lovely old hill,' she exclaimed. 'Can't we write some tale about it? It's full of interest.' In less than a month Elgar had begun to write *Caractacus*, a work which F. Bonavia has described as 'half opera, half cantata, not wholly suited to the concert platform, wholly unsuited to the stage'. The fact is that, as in his other cantatas, Elgar was badly served by his librettist, although the story in itself is not without its possibilities, written as it is around the period when Caractacus had been driven by the Romans towards the Welsh border and had established his camp on the Herefordshire Beacon.

The plot is simple. In Malvern Forest below the camp, Eigen, the daughter of Caractacus, and her minstrel lover Orbin, are met by a Druid maiden and told to warn the King not to seek battle with the Romans. Caractacus then consults a solemn assembly of the Druids, and although their omens are unfavourable the arch-Druid with unexplained treachery persuades him to attack the enemy. His forces are totally defeated, and he returns to the British camp where the Romans take him prisoner, together with his family and Orbin. In the last scene Caractacus appears before the Emperor Claudius, and, despite the clamour of the citizens for the death of the British captive, the Emperor grants him an honourable pardon and permission to remain in Rome.

So far, so good; but the librettist, H. A. Acworth, could not leave well alone, but had to conclude with an inconsequential final chorus extolling the imperial might of Victorian England, under whose sway

> No slave shall be for subject,
>   No trophy wet with tears;
> But folk shall bless the banner,
>   And bless the crosses twin'd,
> That bear the gift of freedom
>   On every blowing wind . . .

There is some splendid music in *Caractacus*, and it is quite remarkable what Elgar can do, even with lines like:

> The gentle wind with kisses kind
>   Is playing on my brow,
> The fawn is leaping round the hind
>   Beneath the rustling bough;

> The dove is cooing to her mate,
> All things in earth appear
> To joy around me while I wait
> For Orbin to be here.

Unfortunately both listeners and performers who would enjoy this expressive music are inescapably faced with the libretto, much of which, one would have thought, must have been embarrassing enough even in imperialistic 1898, although Dr Percy Young has shown that *Caractacus* is highly thought of in Soviet musical circles today as the musical expression of 'the courageous struggle of the British tribes headed by Caractacus against the Roman invader'. This suggests that perhaps one way to make this work acceptable in this country today would be to perform it in translation—in German or Italian, or even in the less familiar Russian—so that the uninspired verse could be forgotten and the music enjoyed for its own sake.

It was at the rehearsals for the first performance of *Caractacus* that W. H. Reed saw Elgar and came under his baton for the first time, and he describes this unforgettable experience in his study of the composer for Dent's Master Musicians series:

> Here was a young lad only just appearing in festival orchestras who, although he had heard a great deal about Elgar and his work, knew very little about either. He was suddenly confronted with a work of the magnitude of *Caractacus* and with the composer himself directing the rehearsal. He cannot recall exactly what he expected to see in this great musician, but he was very much perplexed to see a very distinguished-looking English country gentleman, tall, with a large and somewhat aggressive moustache, a prominent but shapely nose and rather deep-set but piercing eyes. It was his eyes perhaps that gave the clue to his real personality: they sparkled with humour, or became grave or gay, bright or misty as each mood in the music revealed itself. His hands, too, gave another clue: they were never still even when he was not conducting; they moved restlessly, turning up the corners of the pages of the score or giving some indication by a gesture of what he wanted or how he wished a passage to be played; but they were always eloquent, always saying something and giving an inkling of the extreme sensitiveness of his mind and character.
>
> He looked upstanding, had an almost military bearing and

was quite unlike the accepted idea of a musical genius. The orchestra, it is almost needless to say, adored him. From that day to his death every orchestral player privileged to play under his baton or to take part in his works bore him an unquenchable affection. He was practical to a degree, he wasted no time making unnecessary speeches and when he did speak it was always to the point, with few words used to convey his meaning. He obtained all he wanted from his executants by the movements of his delicate and well-shaped hands, by his eyes, which expressed the whole gamut of emotions, and by his whole facial expression, which lit up in an amazing manner when he got the response he desired and when his music throbbed and seethed as he intended that it should. The author was completely overcome by this experience and though he saw him again and again and repeatedly played under his baton in later works he has that first vision indelibly impressed upon his consciousness.

While living in Malvern, Elgar made some of the closest friends of his life, including those who inspired his next work, the *Enigma Variations*, which received its first performance in London under the distinguished conductor Hans Richter, and which firmly established the composer's reputation. Elgar himself has described how the Variations came to be written. One evening after a long and tiring day of teaching he was sitting at the piano consoling himself with a cigar. He then musingly played the 'Enigma' theme as it now stands, and his wife asked him approvingly what it was. 'Nothing,' came the reply, 'but something might be made of it.' He then proceeded to play the theme in various ways and moods suggested by the thought of some of his friends. This was something his wife was sure had never been done before, and so the idea of the *Enigma Variations* took shape.

Fourteen people figure in the Variations, including Elgar himself and his wife, C. A. E. The other Variations suggest the interpretations of the theme which would have been made by friends of his. These are H. D. Steuart-Powell and Basil Nevinson, who played chamber music with him at 'Forli'; W. M. Baker, of Hasfield Court in Gloucestershire; R. P. Arnold, the whimsical and witty son of the poet Matthew Arnold; Isobel Fitton, whose viola playing is illustrated in her Variation; Troyte Griffith, a well-known Malvern architect with whom Elgar shared long country walks; and Winifred Norbury, another musical friend who had given the composer much help in checking the orchestral parts of *Caractacus* for its first performance in Leeds. The organist of Hereford cathedral, G. R. Sinclair—or rather his bulldog Dan— is also represented; and R. B. Townshend, whose soprano falsetto is not forgotten in Variation III. The three asterisks of the thirteenth Variation hide the identity of Lady Mary Lygon, the promoter of the Madresfield Music Festival. Dora Penny (afterwards Mrs Richard Powell) appears as 'Dorabella', and she describes in her book of reminiscences her bewilderment of 'pleasure, pride and almost shame' when she first heard the enchanting music which had been written to represent her. And of course greatest of all there is the music of 'Nimrod', A. J. Jaeger of Novello's, Elgar's 'dear friend, valued adviser and stern critic', whose magnificent Variation has become an indispensable accompaniment of all our great national occasions. It is significant that in the Finale representing himself, Elgar included references to Variation I (his wife) and IX ('Nimrod'), because they were 'the two great influences on his life and art'.

In March 1899 the Elgars moved to a larger, more comfortable detached house on the Wells Road. With his usual passion for word puzzles, Elgar named it 'Craeg Lea', an anagram of E(dward), A(lice) and C(arice) ELGAR. He now had a roomy study with wide views over the Severn plain, and he never tired of pointing out to visitors the infinite variety of changing lights and shadows which passed over the landscape. The house was of course farther away from Great Malvern than 'Forli', but there was a brake, an open horse-drawn vehicle, which passed by at regular intervals, and a Union Jack was displayed if the Elgars wanted it to stop. Mrs Richard Powell has given a lively picture of the composer at this period and of his happy home life, affectionately teasing his young daughter, and keeping up 'a running fire of absurd remarks, comments, chaff and repartee' at meal times, especially when his friend Jaeger was staying with them. During this testing time of his professional life at Malvern, Elgar's wife was more than ever a constant help and inspiration to the composer. As their daughter, Mrs Elgar Blake, has written, 'she gave up her lifelong ambition to be a writer of note because she was so sure that a genius had been given into her charge, and it was her proud responsibility to keep from him every worry and difficulty as far as possible. It was she who ruled the bar lines in all his scores and wrote in the choral parts when required, thereby saving him hours of manual labour; it was she who walked nearly two miles in sunshine or pouring rain to post the precious parcels of MSS. She was the only one who could understand every nuance of his musical intentions and who could, very gently, point out anything that did not absolutely satisfy her; and her advice was taken.'

After the *Enigma Variations*, Elgar's main preoccupation at 'Craeg Lea' was the writing of *The Dream of Gerontius*, which was to bring him international fame and an enthusiastic tribute from Richard Strauss in Germany. In April 1900 Jaeger was excitedly commenting on what Elgar had already written of the new oratorio, saying that nothing so powerful and beautiful had appeared since Wagner's *Parsifal*. Much of the scoring of *Gerontius* was done in the solitude of Birchwood,[1] and when he visited it with Elgar in later years W. H. Reed marvelled that 'such vast things should have come out of this small cottage'. On 6th June Elgar's wife recorded in her diary that *Gerontius* was finished ('Deo gratias'), and on the following day Elgar sent off the completion of the score to Jaeger with the short note: 'God bless you, Nimrod. Here's the end.'

For much of the time he was at 'Craeg Lea', Elgar was still a poor man; on one occasion, for example, he confessed to Jaeger that he could not even afford to send a full score of the *Enigma Variations* to Hans Richter. If it had not been for his wife's income and his earnings from teaching it would have been difficult for them to make both ends meet. Later, however, things began to improve and royalties began to come in more freely, and during his last year in Malvern in 1904 he had the satisfaction of official recognition of his work. He had already been given an honorary Doctorate of Music at Cambridge; now a three-day all-Elgar festival was organized at Covent Garden with the Hallé Orchestra conducted by Hans Richter in the presence of King Edward the Seventh and Queen Alexandra; and he received the honour of a knighthood. By June the Elgars felt that prospects were good enough for them to sell 'Craeg Lea' and move to a much larger house in Hereford, and this brought Elgar's residence in Malvern to an end.

[1] *See* page 140.

It was not of course the end of his associations with the district. He returned again and again, even after they had left Hereford for London; and in 1920, when his 'dear wife and beloved companion' died, it was the quiet churchyard of St Wulstan's Roman Catholic church at Little Malvern, not far from 'Craeg Lea', which he chose for her last resting place; and it was there that his own remains were laid on a snowy February morning some fourteen years later. In an unforeseen way the Malvern Hills also had something of an indirect influence on the recent enthusiastic revival of interest in Elgar's work, because they provided the dramatic scenic background to Ken Russell's brilliant B.B.C. documentary film of the composer's life. When some time ago the readers of the *Observer* were asked for their golden TV memories, this 'Monitor' film was easily if unexpectedly their first choice, and, partly as a result of it, record companies reported an additional boom in the quickened interest already being shown in the symphonies and the violin and 'cello concertos.

In 1929 Sir Barry Jackson, the founder of the Birmingham Repertory Theatre, inaugurated the annual Malvern Festival, which for ten years was not only an act of homage to the dramatist George Bernard Shaw but also the great social event of the town. The first festival presented an impressive programme—*Back to Methuselah*, *Heartbreak House*, *Caesar and Cleopatra*; and also the premier production in England of *The Apple Cart*, Shaw's first play for five years. The London critics travelled down to Malvern on a blisteringly hot Sunday to see the dress rehearsal, and as they sweated uncomfortably in the heat the indefatigable dramatist spent the morning striding over the hills. He always stayed in Malvern for this annual event, and basked in the adulation of his admirers, especially of the ecstatic female *entourage* which he always seemed to attract around him. But although the festival was originally established for the performance of his works it soon included plays by other writers, past and contemporary.

These festivals provided greatly appreciated occasions for Elgar and Shaw to meet, and the two men, so utterly different in so many ways, became close friends. When they first met in 1918 at the London home of Lalla Vandervelde, the wife of a Belgian politician, they took to each other at once, and Shaw was both surprised and flattered that Elgar still remembered the articles on

music which *Corno di Bassetti* [1] had written for the *Star* as long
ago as 1888, and that he could still quote some of their jests and
sallies which even Shaw himself had forgotten.

Shaw had the greatest admiration for Elgar both as man and
composer, and in an article he wrote for the first number of *Music
and Letters* in 1920 he bluntly stated that if he were King or a
Minister of Fine Arts he would award Elgar with an annuity of
one thousand pounds a year on condition that he wrote a symphony every eighteen months. 'Of all English composers,' he
added, 'Elgar is alone for Westminster Abbey.' Elgar recipro-
cated Shaw's esteem, and described him as 'the best friend to any
artist; the kindest and possibly the dearest fellow on earth'.
Barry Jackson seriously thought of bringing these two together
artistically for the first Malvern Festival, and for a while toyed
with the idea of asking Elgar to write an overture to *The Apple
Cart*, but in view of the kind of orchestra that Elgar's music
would have needed, the idea was dropped. Shaw banteringly told
Elgar in mock relief that he was very glad the plan was abandoned
as he feared that the music would have dwarfed the play.

From 1932 onwards, all except three of Shaw's new plays had
their world *première* at Malvern. In this particular year the new
play was *Too True to be Good*, and Barry Jackson had arranged for
the critics to be brought from London by air, a gesture which
might have been splendid publicity, but which unfortunately mis-
fired badly, for when the day arrived flying conditions were so
hazardous that the flight had to be delayed. The start of the play
was held up in Malvern for over an hour, but still the critics had
not arrived, and it was decided to start without them. Half way
through the second act they stumbled into the theatre after a
flight so bumpy that most of them had been painfully air-sick.
They were helped to their seats but, more dead than alive, they
were quite incapable of following any play with intelligent
attention, least of all a new one of which they had already missed
one act and a half. Barry Jackson's bright idea on this occasion
proved a disastrous mistake.

In this same year Elgar was seriously thinking of writing an
opera, and he asked Shaw if he would provide the libretto. Shaw
wisely declined, pointing out that his plays had 'a verbal music of

---

[1] Shaw's *nom de plume* for the articles.

their own', which would make a strange counterpoint for Elgar's music. Elgar then consulted Barry Jackson, who proved sympathetic and helpful, and agreed after some initial doubts to write a libretto based on an obscure play by Ben Jonson which Elgar had decided was the perfect subject for his opera. During 1933, the seventy-six year old composer worked enthusiastically at *The Spanish Lady*, as the opera was to be called, and also at a third symphony which had been commissioned by the B.B.C. Shaw had been an energetic supporter of both these new works, the first major works Elgar had planned since the death of his wife in 1920. Soon the composer was playing extracts from both symphony and opera to Shaw and his wife when they visited him at his last home at Marl Bank in Worcester, but the works were never completed. In February of the following year Elgar died, leaving behind him only tantalizing scraps of the music that might have been.

Shaw was to outlive him by some sixteen years, and continued to be the central figure of the Malvern Festival until 1939. That year saw the first production of his *In Good King Charles's Golden Days*, which some critics considered his best play since *Saint Joan*; but the festival carried on in an ominous atmosphere of international uncertainty. On the third day of September the storm broke; Britain was once again plunged into the cataclysm of war, and the Malvern festivals came to an end.

In 1977 another and much more elaborate revival of the Festival was undertaken, planned largely around Elgar's music and Shaw's plays. This revival has been a great success and the new yearly Malvern Festival has a promising future.

CHAPTER FIVE

The Seven Sisters

No LESS than seven Malverns are strung along the roads which encircle the hills. West Malvern alone faces the Herefordshire border; the rest, Malvern Link, North Malvern, Great Malvern, South Malvern (more commonly known as the Wyche), Malvern Wells and Little Malvern, stretch down the eastern side from north to south. Great Malvern is easily the capital of them all, both by size and importance, but it is a town of comparatively recent growth. Writing one hundred and fifty years ago Chambers states that it then consisted of only about fifty houses. Thus it is primarily a Victorian town, apart from the occasional exception like the seventeenth-century coaching inn the Unicorn, the Regency Foley Arms built round about 1810 and the gracious Mount Pleasant Hotel of a somewhat earlier date.

To see the impressively bold fashion in which buildings climb dizzily up the sides of the hills at Great Malvern, North Malvern and parts of Malvern Wells is to appreciate how adroitly the architects took advantage of the dramatic back-cloth of the hills, and the solidity of Malvern rock for a foundation. In her interesting book, *The Silhouette of Malvern*, Catherine Moody shows how these unusual sites which bring 'the whole height of a building to one's notice' have influenced the character of the building here:

> In Malvern one is forced to look uphill at such an angle that heights are foreshortened, or down over the roofs of buildings below. Looking down from St Ann's Road one can see right on to the roofs of the houses and, which is most fascinating to a newcomer, right into the tops of the chimney pots. No wonder then that the buildings of Malvern abound in elaborate roof features when roofs are brought so closely to one's notice.

Even private houses have an unusual proliferation of domes, belfries and spires. The belvedere of Aldwyn Tower, to be seen from afar, proclaims the revivalist spirit which pervaded the town. Link Tower Lodge has a similar belvedere. The Link School building—a red brick reminiscent of a castle on the Rhine—is turreted and towered. Transplanted from their age and setting turrets and towers do not serve to conjure up thoughts of mysterious antiquity and romantic legend, although that was without doubt what the architects had hoped to do. In the case of the Link School, originally built as the Station Hotel, the owners had hoped to do this whilst at the same time serving the needs of the hungry and thirsty trippers from the Black Country.

For those who are fascinated by Victoriana, Malvern is full of treasures, and we can start at the station with its splendid suggestion of ecclesiastical architecture exploited in iron, including curiously wrought cast-iron capitals around the pillars supporting the platform roof. The coming of the railway to Malvern in the second half of the nineteenth century was bound to have its effect on the town, and now that the palmy days of the locomotive have passed it is impossible not to feel more than a touch of nostalgia for the lively spirit and assiduous enterprise of the 'Railway Age' which could lavish such care on details in even such a small station as this. No one has recorded recollections of trains which have now vanished from Malvern more vividly than George Sayer in *Age Frater*, the Malvern College Centenary Book:

> Time, the Diesel and Dr Beeching have between them drastically altered the Malvern railway scene. The L.M.S. local, for example, which used to depart from the Great Malvern siding and meander on its way through Upton to Ashchurch, has long ceased to run; the line beyond the Wells junction is now a straight green lane, a possible problem for archaeologists in the remote future. On warm sunny afternoons its Emmett-like tank engine and single maroon coach used to glide modestly past the swimming bath with scarcely a puff. By contrast the G.W.R. push-me-pull-you, now also defunct, seemed fussy and self-important.
>
> Those were the days of vast double-headed Sunday excursion trains from the Black Country and Birmingham. After unloading their family parties they laboured up the Wells siding, with many a false start, and then rested until it

was time to slide down and take up the day-trippers, now footsore, hot and disillusioned after trailing straight up and down the side of the hills, poor things.

In the roads between the station and the town centre you can spend happy hours discovering a bewildering number of different styles of nineteenth-century domestic architecture. Here is Victorian Gothic in plenty—castellated houses with gables and battlements; towers, turrets and spires; pointed arches and oriel windows; and there is even a sprinkling of Caledonian baronial, pastiche Flemish and Ruskinian Venetian. Priory Road, Abbey Road and Avenue Road are especially rewarding; as Miss Moody happily puts it, these roads are 'a museum of architectural features from famous monuments of medieval architecture from England and the Continent'.

There are other surprises too—a few beautifully proportioned cast-iron Victorian pillar-boxes still in use, and an embattled Gothic butcher's shop beside the priory gateway. The infinite variety of Victorian buildings in Malvern certainly provides endless pleasure for the connoisseur, and it is salutary to reflect that these architectural vagaries, which only a generation ago were dismissed as vulgar eccentricities, can now be regarded with this affectionate nostalgia; it is realized that they do represent a past age of undeniable energy, vitality and originality. 'The greatness of the Victorian Age', writes Robert Furneaux Jordan, 'is of a different kind from the greatness of other periods. That adds to rather than detracts from its fascination . . . and that fascination is to be found as much in the age's architecture as in anything else.'

The framework of Great Malvern's layout is provided by the Wells Road and Worcester Road running north to south high up along the flank of the hills, and Church Street which climbs up sharply to join them at right angles in Belle Vue Terrace. North of Church Street there is a series of roads lying parallel to Worcester Road; to the south the network of roads spreads around in a more complicated fashion. By Belle Vue Terrace there are the Rose Bank gardens which offer the attractions of a small intimate park combined with a fine view over the priory church tower. A short distance farther on there are the buildings already mentioned—the Mount Pleasant Hotel, with its well-proportioned Orangery, the Unicorn and the Foley Arms. Another building which stands out is Barclay's Bank, once the library and boarding-house of the nineteenth-century Malvern Spa. The former baths and pump-room building is now occupied by various business firms; Mr Beard's 'genteely fitted up' Belle Vue Hotel has been transformed into a row of shops; and Lloyd's Bank now stands on the site of the old Crown which Dr Wilson took over and re-named Graefenberg House for his water-cure establishment. At the end of a short cul-de-sac beside the Congregational church is a private house, Holly Mount, where the young Princess Victoria spent a holiday in 1830 with her mother, the rustling, bustling, voluble Duchess of Kent. For many years one of the Malvern donkeys bore a badge of distinction on its bridle and was given the name 'Royal' Moses as a reward for carrying the future Queen of England up to the top of Worcestershire Beacon, but the recollection of the Duchess of Kent's ample figure prompts the thought that it was her donkey which should have received the grateful reward rather than Moses, who, after all, was carrying only a small eleven-year-old child.

In Church Street the shops mostly have the dull unimaginative fronts which you can see repeated *ad nauseam* in every town, and which are so uninteresting when compared, say, with Malvern's Gothic butcher, but I never fail to notice in this street the little pub with the odd name Fermor Arms. The Fermor Arms and adjoining properties have since been demolished.

Malvern's greatest treasure, with her hills, is the priory church. It is sad that the public-spirited villagers who saved the church from destruction in the sixteenth century could not afford to buy the land on the west and south sides, so that now an hotel's private property enjoys what should be the parishioners' most satisfying view of the church as a whole. Fortunately the existing north entrance has the pleasant foreground of an extensive churchyard, shaded by some fine trees. Outside the east end it is still possible to see where the fourteenth-century Lady Chapel and a Norman crypt once stood before their destruction at the time of the dissolution of the monastery. Fragments of stone-work that remain show that the chapel's Decorated style was still untouched and had not been included in the great rebuilding activity of the fifteenth century, but today from the outside it is difficult to imagine that the whole of the church is anything but a fine example of Perpendicular work, the design of the richly panelled tower being so obviously based on its prototype at Gloucester Cathedral. Even the nineteenth-century porch was rebuilt in the same style as its fifteenth-century predecessor, so it is all the more of a surprise to be confronted inside by the sturdy Norman pillars of the nave which contrast so strikingly with the Perpendicular style of the unusually large clerestory and the ceiling. A second feature which immediately strikes the eye is the difference in width of the two aisles. During the rebuilding the north aisle was widened, but the now blocked-up Norman door in the south aisle, which once led into the cloisters, shows how near the monastery buildings were, and this made it impossible for the builders to enlarge this aisle in the same way.

A full description of the church would need a small book to itself, and the reader would be well advised to procure the excellent guides available in the church. Here I will merely make a personal choice of a few special features which I can see again and again with ever increasing enjoyment.

What remains of the ancient stained glass in the great east window can only be adequately appreciated with the aid of a pair of binoculars, which will reveal the beauty and variety of the colours—the reds and blues (especially the blues) and the contrasting shades of silvery white and golden yellow. The radiant splendour of this medieval craftsmanship makes us regret all the more bitterly the criminal neglect and vandalism which reduced so much loveliness to these precious fragments. The equally magnificent west window was, according to an old tradition, the gift of Richard the Third. It once held a representation of the Last Judgment, but is now filled with ancient glass from other parts of the church. In the north side of the choir the window representing the legend of St Werstan [1] is of special interest, and in the north aisle, as a contrast and a curiosity, a window commemorates Queen Victoria's Jubilee and shows her receiving the news of her accession; her coronation; and her Jubilee service where she is depicted with no less a person than Kaiser William in the background—surely a unique English ecclesiastical setting for a portrait of that strange megalomaniacal German ruler.

[1] *See* page 7.

It has already been seen that Malvern's Benedictine monks spent much of their time in long and continually recurring services. For these protracted religious exercises the one small gesture to the frailties of the flesh was the 'misericord', a device which permitted the seat of a stall to be turned up, revealing a small ledge against which a monk could lean without breaking the rule by actually sitting down. Indeed 'should the worshipper be so negligent as to fall into a slumber, a thing not always guarded against even amongst monks, the seat would thrust him forward, slam down, and so expose his indolence'.

The last three nearest the altar in each row are modern, but twenty-two of the original twenty-four ancient carvings below the ledges are still in existence. Executed with skill and lively imagination, they show a remarkable variety of subjects ranging from the humorous and grotesque to near-the-bone satirical. Twelve of the seats had carvings representing the months of the year, but of these only ten survive. The following is the full list of the subjects, starting in each case from the west side, moving towards the altar:

NORTH SIDE (left facing altar), FRONT ROW:

1. A figure seated at a table holding a large cup in each hand; probably a representation of *January*. The supporting side carvings are two heraldic Tudor roses.

2. A labourer weeding and using a double-pronged staff, a 'crotch', in one hand, to bend the weed over, and in the other hand a sickle-shaped 'weed-hook' to cut it; probably a representation of *April*. The supporters are a pair of long-clawed wood pigeons.

3. Three mice (or are they rats?) triumphantly hanging a cat on a gallows. It is a realistic satirical representation of the 'biter bit', and the open mouth and bulging eyes of the expiring cat are a good example of the carver's skill. The supporters are two owls which, if the executioners are mice, give extra piquancy to the satire.

4. A man with luxuriant curls scything grass and representing haymaking in *June*.

5. A man carrying a basket of fruit on one arm, and in his other hand holding an enormous bunch of grapes. *September*.

6. A representation of the cockatrice or basilisk, the fabulous reptile which was supposedly hatched by a serpent from a cock's egg, and which could shrivel the beholder with its breath and gaze. It is appropriately shown with a cock's head and breast, and a long, dragon-like tail, but it has a remarkably benevolent expression for a beast with such a reputation.

NORTH SIDE, BACK ROW:

1. A lion, looking rather like a mastiff—probably representing *July*.
2. A swineherd knocking down acorns, with two boars as supporters. *October*.
3. This carving has been repaired at some time and was replaced upside-down. It appears to show a drunkard being beaten by his wife. Another figure is prone on the floor still drinking.
4. Two long-necked grotesques, one with claws and the other with webbed feet.
5. A hen-pecked husband scene representing *February*. The wife has returned from the well with her pitcher and is hitting her husband on the head with her distaff as he kneels to take off her boots.
6. A man sowing with a sack of corn beside him and a basket slung over his shoulder. On each side is a pigeon. *March*.

SOUTH SIDE (right facing altar), FRONT ROW:

1. A mummer's mask with supporters that might well represent Comedy and Tragedy.
2. The face of a man with an almost Gioconda-like smile.
3. A man killing an ox so vigorously that his pole-axe has been broken. *December*.
4. An angel wearing a cope and playing a cithern, the lute-like instrument which was the ancestor of the modern guitar.
5. A 'wyvern', the heraldic bat-winged, two-legged dragon with barbed tail.
6. A man carrying two great bunches of flowers, probably in a Rogation-tide procession and so representing *May*.

SOUTH SIDE, BACK ROW:

1. Two grotesque figures, one with a monk's cowl, the other
   with what appears to be a duck's head. One suggestion is that
   this illustrates a now forgotten satire about monk and layman
   relationships.
2. A merman and mermaid, the former holding a mirror, and the
   latter a comb.
3. A man in bed supported by his wife; a doctor is holding two
   flasks of urine for examination. This was a much favoured
   method of diagnosis in medieval times, as readers of Shake-
   speare will recall.[1]
4. A monk drives away a devil by applying a pair of bellows
   somewhat indelicately to a man's posterior.
5. and 6. The carvings of the next two stalls are missing; possibly
   they were too coarse for nineteenth-century purists and
   suffered the fate of two similar misericords in Bristol Cathedral
   which were removed and burnt.

We have seen that Malvern's manufacture of encaustic tiles
became quite a considerable industry for the monastery, and it is
not surprising that many of its best examples are to be found in
the priory church where there still remain more than a thousand
with some hundred different designs. The tiles on the sides of the
sanctuary and the floors of the church are, of course, garish nineteenth-century imitations, but the originals are to be found on
both sides of the reredos, on the semicircular wall of the ambu-
latory behind the altar, and in the north aisle on the low wall
screening the sanctuary. Some of these ancient tiles bear Christian
symbols like the fish and the pelican; some show armorial
bearings or mottoes; and others are obviously merely ornamental in design. Three subjects which can be found and identi-
fied without much difficulty are of special interest. One bears the
inscription, *Mentem sanctam, spontaneum honorem Deo, et patrie
liberacionem* ('[Pray for] a holy mind, ready honour to God, and
deliverance for your country.'). For some inexplicable reason this
prayer was regarded as an infallible spell against fire. Another set
of four is called 'the lepers' tile' and bears the names of the four
Evangelists and the inscription, *Miseremini mei, saltem vos amici*

[1] e.g. Falstaff's question in *Henry IV*, 2, I. ii.

mei, quia manus Domini tetigit me ('Have pity on me, at least you my friends, because the hand of God hath touched me.'). A third, 'the executor's tile', has an inscription of eight lines:

Thanke mon yi liffe
mai not eu endure
yat yow dost yi self
of yat yow kepist
un to yi sectur cure
an eu hit availe ye
hit is but aventure.

which has been rendered in modern English as:

Think, man, thy life
May not ever endure;
That thou doest thyself
Of that thou are sure;
But that thou entrustest
Unto thy executor's care,
And whether it avail thee
It is but chance.

It was a salutary reminder to the reader that he would not live for ever, and that, as he could not be certain his executor would carry out his wishes, it would be well to make over his gift to the Church during his lifetime instead of by legacy in his will.

The tomb of Walcher, Malvern's second prior, was moved in the eighteenth century, and its stone coffin lid now lies within a recessed chantry in St Anne's Chapel on the south side of the church. It has a Latin inscription which has been translated as:

In this tomb lies the body of DOCTOR WALCHER, a native of the dukedom of Lorraine and Prior of this Convent. He was an acute Philosopher, and able Astrologer, a Geometrician and Mathematician, a pious Christian and a humble Monk. His death is universally regretted both by the Clergy and Laity. He died the first of October in the year of our Lord 1135. Let every Christian earnestly pray that his Soul may live in Heaven.

Beside Walcher's coffin lid is another battered stone slab which belonged to the coffin of the ill-fated Prior Wykewane, whose appointment by the Bishop of Worcester precipitated the unseemly scandal of the 'William of Ledbury affair'.[1]

[1] *See* page 10.

Lying above this chantry, but best seen from the choir, is the magnificent Knotsford monument set up by their daughter Anne, who kneels at a prie-dieu beside it. Her four sisters are represented on both sides of the monument, which shows life-size figures of John Knotsford dressed in Elizabethan armour and his wife Jane in ruff, long embroidered gown and dainty shoes. The figures are carved in alabaster, and are so well preserved that even the smallest details of contemporary costume and armour can still be clearly seen.

The priory gateway is all that remains of the monastery buildings which were once the centre of Malvern. On its south side there is some not particularly comely brick-work, but the north side, although much restored and much reduced from its original size, still gives some idea of the dignified welcome a stranger would have had when asking for shelter and hospitality. The posts and fragments of the hinges of the old gates can still be seen, and on the right the small window of what was once the porter's lodge. As the gates of the monastery were closed by day and night, except for the brethren or their guests to pass in and out, this window enabled the porter to speak with any stranger before admitting him.

Close by in Abbey Road are the Festival Theatre and Winter Gardens. Tudor Edwards has asserted that 'it is locally claimed that the Winter Gardens is built in the style of the Italian Renaissance', and he adds rather spitefully: 'One begins to feel sorry for the Italian Renaissance.' In fact both the theatre and the Winter Gardens are pleasant enough, although it is depressing to see that the fountain in the Pump Room no longer works. Behind is Priory Park which with its trees, flowers and bathing-pool is one of the more obvious attractions of the town.

College Road leads to Malvern's famous public school, one of the many Victorian public schools founded in the first flush of enthusiasm for Arnold's reformed Rugby. Malvern was a comparative latecomer to this burst of educational activity, but the date of its foundation, 1862, was a significantly prosperous time in the history of the Malvern water cure, and the recent successful foundation of Cheltenham College demonstrated the advantages of establishing a school at a spa town. Malvern had its own share of retired Indian civil servants and army colonels 'who "nourished the fleeting remnants of their livers" on the hills and by the springs, and who wanted to provide a public school cheaper and nearer home than the old public schools'.[1]

In his *History of Malvern College*—an important sidelight on the evolution of the Victorian public schools in general as well as a history of the college—Ralph Blumenau has traced the story of its foundation, its vicissitudes and its successes up to the present day. The school was started with a capital of twenty-four thousand pounds raised by subscriptions to a limited company, Malvern College Limited. The statements of its objects echoed the terms of most other prospectuses of these 'new' public schools—'the establishment and conduct of a college as nearly as possible on the model of the great public schools, for the sons of gentlemen'. It was to give 'sound religious, classical, mathematical and general education of the highest order, in strict conformity with the principles of the Church of England'. Charles Francis Hansom, brother of Joseph Aloysius Hansom who invented the famous cab, was chosen as the architect of the new school; a safe choice, as he had already built Clifton College in the neo-Gothic style which, as John Betjeman has remarked, was believed to convey both the Christian nature of the education provided within its walls and the atmosphere of Oxford and Cambridge, for which the public schools were a preparation.[2] Hansom's design is undeniably impressive with its massive tower (which manifestly owes much to the Lupton Tower at Eton) standing out against the steeply rising background of the hills. Later buildings, like the chapel and the Memorial Library, were designed by other architects, but Hansom's original building set the medieval-style pattern which, with qualified developments, has been followed by his successors.

In a chapter covering the headmastership of H. C. A. Gaunt, Mr Blumenau describes the college's two sudden enforced evacuations during the war, first to Blenheim Palace and then (after a short-lived return to Malvern) to Harrow in order to allow the Telecommunications Research Establishment to occupy their buildings. It is a remarkable story of agonized decisions boldly taken, seemingly insuperable difficulties overcome, and tenacious courage, tolerance and faith shown by masters and boys alike. It

[1] *Victoria County History of Worcestershire.*
[2] *Centenary Essays on Clifton College.*

is equally revealing to read how rapidly the school renewed itself when it finally returned to its rightful home.

Malvern College's reputation as one of the most progressive public schools in the country is firmly established and although, like all other public schools, it faces a future unpredictable and uncertain in these days when political considerations meddle so closely with education, yet 'they feel confident', as Ralph Blumenau puts it, 'that schools like Malvern can . . . have as much to contribute as ever they had. They hope that when changes come, as come they will, they will not for political reasons destroy but rather maintain and enlarge what is educationally valuable in the public school system. Malvern will welcome any changes that will enable it to go on playing a worth-while part in a rapidly changing world'.

The other Malverns can most conveniently be taken in order, going northwards around the hills. Malvern Link lies on the northern outskirts of Great Malvern and is far enough away to enjoy a more satisfying view of the hills. J. Lees-Milne in his book on Worcestershire pays a well-deserved tribute to the Church of the Ascension in Somers Park for its dignified simplicity and because 'thought and craftsmanship are apparent in design and execution of every part of the church'. He writes equally enthusiastically of the late nineteenth-century Chapel of the Convent belonging to the Sisters of the Holy Name in Ranelagh Road as 'the work of a master', in spite of its somewhat forbidding exterior of harsh red brick. 'The interior is superb Perpendicular, light and almost gay. White hooded nuns, like pools of moonshine, kneel in unexpected places.' The chapel may be visited only by special permission, but those who have had the privilege of seeing it cannot fail to have been like myself dazzled and delighted by its lovely, lofty, cool white beauty.

There is little of interest to be seen in North Malvern Road, which follows the contours of North Hill into West Malvern Road. West Malvern itself enjoys a high altitude, splendid views to the west and unforgettable sunsets behind the Welsh mountains. St James's School for girls stands out unmistakably beside the road; much of its handsome building was once the stately mansion belonging to Lady Howard de Walden. The modern church of St James near by is a spacious dignified building worthy of its fine situation.

In an interesting article which appeared a short time ago in *The Gloucestershire Countryside*, Mary Quartley has traced a hitherto unknown link between West Malvern and the playwright James Barrie. It all began when an eighteen-year-old girl, Lilian Norrie, wrote to him from South Africa in 1916, sending him some of her writings for his criticism and telling him she was planning to travel to England. Barrie was impressed by the girl's enthusiasm, but he advised her not to come to this country during one of the worst years of the First World War. Disregarding his advice Lilian Norrie arrived in London, and Barrie arranged for her to live in West Malvern, away from the danger of air raids. She remained in the district all her life and 'never left even for one day to go to London'. At regular intervals she posted manuscripts to Barrie, who had them typed at his own expense from her hand-writing in order to be able to read them, and he continued to send her his critical advice and friendly encouragement.

The young exile from South Africa never married, but she made a number of good friends in Malvern and finally settled down with a Miss Prichard, who lived in a secluded house on the western slopes of the hills with three maids and two Siamese cats. 'Miss Norrie was something of an enigma,' writes Mary Quartley. She never succeeded in getting anything published but she did become the adopted daughter of Miss Prichard and inherited her estate. One of the many manuscripts she sent to Barrie for his comments was about 'the waiting land', and Mrs Quartley makes the interesting suggestion that this may have given Barrie the idea of the 'island that liked to be visited' in *Mary Rose*.

After leaving West Malvern the road traces a course along a shelf of the western side of the hills with an extensive view over Herefordshire. After passing the Wyche cutting, Jubilee Drive gives more and more panoramic, sweeping views until you reach the Herefordshire Beacon, and the road from Ledbury dips north-wards down past Wynd's Point. It was here about ninety years ago that the famous singer Jenny Lind bought two old cottages in the disused quarry beside the British Camp Hotel, and gradually rebuilt them into the beautiful house which was to be her last home and which was her special delight for the last ten years of her life.[1] The 'Swedish Nightingale', as she was affectionately

[1] It is now a private house and is not open to the public.

called in England, and her husband, Otto Goldschmidt, had been living in England since 1858, but they had moved from house to house. Here at Wynd's Point she at last found a countryside she fell in love with, and a house and a garden she could make and tend among 'the oldest rocks this earth can boast'.

By the time she settled here, Jenny Lind had officially given up public singing, but in 1883 a railway porter who was carrying her luggage from the train at Great Malvern station plucked up courage and asked her if she would honour them by singing at a concert for the Railwaymen's Benevolent Fund at Malvern. To his intense surprise and gratification she consented, and her very last public appearance was at this 'Railway Concert'.

When she died four years later after a long illness, and was buried in Great Malvern cemetery, she was mourned by the shop-keepers and the cottagers of the district where she had made her last home, as well as by the Queen and by friends and admirers throughout the world, for whom that glorious, full-toned soprano, that warm, vivid personality and that vigorous, generous disposition were now no more than a memory, and a memory especially real to those who had been fortunate enough to know her at the height of her powers.

Little Malvern is aptly named, for it is the smallest of all the Malverns, hardly more than a hamlet. Magnificently situated at the foot of Herefordshire Beacon is all that remains of the priory—the Court, and the tower and choir of the priory church which now form the nave and chancel of the parish church. This Benedictine priory had a somewhat chequered history, and perhaps it is not surprising that one of its monks figures in the legend of Ragged Stone Hill.[1] Founded in the twelfth century, it was under the authority of the great Benedictine monastery at Worcester which had the right to choose its prior, and 'in way of correction' could remove monks from Little Malvern to Worcester and transfer monks from Worcester in their place. The priory was always very small, and its very remoteness in the depths of Malvern Forest seemed to make it difficult to control even from Worcester. After about one hundred and fifty years of apparently uneventful existence, its monks figure in the records when a stern condemnation of their lax and slovenly ways was issued by

[1] *See* page 92.

Bishop Cobham of Worcester. There was even something more seriously amiss than just laxity of discipline, for 'the voice of scandal was not unheard, and once a prior was enjoined to admit a certain Brother Hugh de Pyribrok to purgation respecting a charge of immorality. It is to be hoped that Brother Hugh was able to clear himslf of the imputation as he became prior himself a few years later.' [1] At all events Bishop Cobham's censure seems to have had some effect, because there is no evidence of any further disciplinary troubles for another century and a half when in 1480 Bishop Alcock came over from Worcester in person to visit the priory, and was so shocked by 'the great ruin of the church and place' that he dismissed the Prior and sent the monks 'by reason of their demerits' to Gloucester for correction. Meanwhile Alcock set about rebuilding the neglected ruinous church and conventual buildings. After two years he was able to write: 'I have builded your Church and your place of lodging is also sufficiently repaired,' and the penitent and rehabilitated monks were allowed to return to Little Malvern under a new prior. The restored priory resumed its presumably reformed way of life for another half century, and then was dissolved like the rest of the lesser monasteries. The priory buildings and land were ultimately sold to the Russells, and a branch of the family still owns the Court, part of which is all that remains of the old monastic buildings. It was a stipulation of the sale that the tower and choir of the church should be preserved for the use of the parishioners; the rest of the church became ruinous through a combination of neglect and despoliation.

Inside there are few remains of the original Norman church which Bishop Alcock rebuilt. The east window was once filled with figures of Edward IV, his queen and their family. All that you can now see in this once splendid window are the kneeling figure of the ill-fated Edward Prince of Wales, who was later to be murdered with his brother in the Tower, and to whom Bishop Alcock was tutor; part of the figure of the Queen, Elizabeth Woodville and her four elder daughters; and part of the figure of Bishop Alcock himself. Unfortunately the misericord carvings of the monks' stalls have been hacked away, but the handrests have survived, and one of them gives a good representation of two pigs feeding from a trough. The tiles on the floor of the sanctuary

[1] *Victoria County History of Worcestershire.*

are similar to those at Great Malvern and were obviously fired in the same kiln. They are badly worn, but it is just possible to identify the 'executor's tile', and the 'fire spell', and the 'lepers' tile'.

There is something particularly appealing about Little Malvern Priory and the ruined remains of its transepts and chapels. It is a place full of authentic atmosphere where the past seems to over-whelm the present, especially at the fall of the year when

> Coldly, sadly descends
> The autumn evening. The field
> Strewn with its dark yellow drifts
> Of wither'd leaves, and the elms,
> Fade into darkness apace,
> Silent. . . .

No other place I know recalls to me certain poetry so vividly— Milton's *Il Penseroso*, Coleridge's *Christabel*, or perhaps even more suitably the rich melancholy of Keats's *The Eve of St Agnes* with its haunting concluding stanza.

The best view of Little Malvern Court is obtained from the lane above it. From here you can see the fascinating 'pepper-box' turret and the long yew hedge which is so splendidly clipped into various ornamental shapes. The Court is the original of the house described in the introductory chapter of one of the earliest of the nineteenth-century mystical 'problem novels', J. H. Short-house's once popular *John Inglesant*, which tells the story of a young seventeenth-century Englishman torn between the conflicting claims of Roman Catholicism and Protestantism.[1] The book opens with a description of the

old and very picturesque house, jumbled together with the additions of many centuries, from the round tower-like staircase with an extinguisher turret, to a handsome addition of two or three years ago. Close by was the mutilated tower of a ruined priory, the chancel of which is used as the parish church. A handsome stone wing of one storey, built in the early Gothic style, and not long completed, formed the entrance hall and dining-room, with a wide staircase at the back. The hall was profusely hung with old landscapes and family portraits. After a short introduction to my friend's family, we were soon assembled in the newly finished

[1] Plowden Hall in Shropshire is another suggested 'original'.

dining-room, with its stone walls and magnificent over-hanging Gothic fireplace. The room was hung entirely with portraits, several of them being ecclesiastics in different religious costumes, contrasting, to my eyes, strangely with the gay cavaliers and the beautiful ladies of the Stuarts' Court, and not less elaborately dressed portraits of the last century, and with those of my host and hostess in the costume of the Regency. I was struck with the portrait which happened to be opposite me, of a young man with a tonsured head, in what appeared to me to be a simple monk's dress, and I asked the Priest, a beautiful and mild-looking old man, whom it was intended to represent.

A short distance along the Wells Road is St Wulstan's Roman Catholic church. Here Lady Elgar's funeral service was held in 1920, and in its small gallery four of his friends played the slow movement from Elgar's String Quartet which his wife had loved so well. Elgar himself is buried beside his wife in the graveyard behind the church. These simple surroundings for the grave of the greatest English composer since Purcell are perhaps appropriate, but the ramshackle, broken-down garage which greets the visitor at the entrance to the graveyard is inexcusable, and provoked some unprintable remarks from an American admirer of Elgar's music whom I met recently. The grave bears the inscription:

Pray for the Soul of
Caroline Alice
LADY ELGAR
only Daughter of the late
Sir Henry Gee Roberts, K.C.B.
of Hazeldine House
Worcestershire
The dearly beloved
and revered Wife
of Edward Elgar Kt.
She died at Hampstead
April 7th, 1920
R. I. P.
In memory also
of the above named
EDWARD ELGAR
Born June 2nd, 1857
Died Feb. 23rd, 1934

Holy Well Road is a turning off Wells Road and goes past the old Wells House, now a preparatory school. It was here in 1881 that the brilliant medievalist and pugnacious eccentric G. G. Coulton began to earn his living. Unlike an earlier great man, who deplored the life of a beggarly usher as 'the last refuge of inefficiency and despair', Coulton was rightly persuaded that 'the healthy little humiliations of a schoolmaster's life are part of an ideal educational system for every University student before matriculation'. Coulton was fortunate to start teaching in such beautiful surroundings and under such an able headmaster, and he acknowledges this in characteristic terms in his autobiography *Fourscore Years*.

The Wells House at Malvern Wells, some two miles south of Great Malvern, is a large white building high up on the slope of the hills: so high and so big that it can be seen with the naked eye from Severn bank at Worcester, ten miles distant. The Reverend William Wilberforce Gedge had taken a lease of this house and founded there a solid and well-respected Preparatory School of some thirty boys. . . . Gedge himself was an excellent man for his job . . . vigorous, upright, broad-shouldered, looking in his frock-coat the very type of that prosperous Victorian figure which Max Beerbohm has drawn for his inimitable triptych in the Fitzwilliam Museum. He always came down to breakfast with a vigour which contrasted, though not too crudely, with our less exuberant energies, damped by an hour of class work. . . . Exuding vitality from every pore, before attacking breakfast proper he always needed a glass of cold Malvern water, purest in Britain as it gushes from the hard volcanic syenite. . . .

My own classroom had a magnificent view. Just at our feet, the village and its two hotels. First, the 'Hornyold Arms', called after the ancient Roman Catholic family who owned the whole estate and had their ancestral hall some three miles off down the plain. Then, the Essington Hotel, with an enormous whiteheart cherry tree, glorious alike in spring and summer and autumn. In good years, all through June, a gipsy family encamped under the tree with their antique shot-guns, hired to keep off the birds by some fruiterer who had contracted to buy the whole crop. It was parent perhaps of the many self-sown cherries which splash all the hill-woods of Malvern Wells with orange and crimson in the autumn. The Wells House looked out due east but one had only to climb the steep slope on which it stood and there was a western prospect no less enchanting in its own way.

Since this was written the Holy Well has been most splendidly restored by Mr John Parkes who financed the whole project himself. This is a fine example of what enthusiasm and good taste can do to save a legacy of the past which is of historic value.

Where Holy Well Road rejoins Wells Road there is the oldest building in Malvern Wells, the Ruby. It is an attractive eighteenth-century house with prominent bow windows, and by its name is linked with Admiral Benbow, the seventeenth-century sea-dog whose courage and tenacity on active service were acknowledged even by his French adversaries. The *Ruby* was indeed the name of the Admiral's last ship, but the tradition that he lived in this house is not correct. It is much more likely that another member of the same family, Richard Benbow, whose monument is in Great Malvern's priory church, was responsible for giving the house its name and also suggested the sign of The Admiral Benbow which formerly graced the present Hornyold Arms. The other hotel here, the Essington, was well known in the heyday of the nineteenth-century spa, and Chambers recalls that one of its guests was moved to poetical effusion with the lines:

At Malvern Wells where health bears the belle,
All visitors notice the famous hotel
By Essington kept, where you meet with good cheer,
Good wines and good liquours, good ale and good beer.
Of damp beds and rough treatment no person's in danger,
Whilst civil attention is paid to each stranger;
Then honour the house if you please, if you call
The Essingtons cheerly will wait on you all.
To serve you with zeal, and obey each behest,
They'll endeavour to please you by doing their best.

Some way farther along the Wells Road is 'Craeg Lea', where Elgar lived for some eight years, and then by Rose Bank Gardens there is a notice which announces '99 Steps to Saint Ann's Well'. I personally have never counted the number of steps, but you would be ill-advised to imagine that at the end of the steps you have arrived at the well. There is quite a long, steep, zigzag path to follow, but it is worth the climb, and in summer it is green, shady and cool even on the hottest day. The well water gushes out of a pipe beside the small cottage well-house which also dispenses it in a marble basin presented in 1892 by the formidable 'Lord of the Manor', Lady Emily Foley, who also commissioned the inscription engraved above it:

> Drink of this crystal fountain
> And praise the loving Lord,
> Who from the rocky mountain
> This living stream outpoured,
> Fit emblems of the holy fount
> That flows from God's Eternal Mount.

It is pleasant to find that at least this old well survives of all the wells which once made Malvern famous, and even more pleasant to see how many people, young and not so young, climb up to see it. The old dictum says *laborare est orare* ('to work is to pray'). A corollary might be *ascendere est orare* ('climbing is a prayer'), or perhaps it should be *ascendere est laborare*.

CHAPTER SIX

On Malvern Ridge

ONE of the many pleasures and advantages of walking on the
Malverns is that with some twenty-six miles of footpaths there is
an almost endless variety of alternative routes at the walker's
disposal. There are easy paths, gentle climbs and stiffer gradients,
and for most of the hills there is a choice of beginning and ending
a walk in so many different areas. The motorist and cyclist too
are both offered unusually varied scenery along the roads which
girdle the hills—the eastern side from Great Malvern to Wynd's
Point at the foot of the Herefordshire Beacon; the western side
from West Malvern over the Jubilee Drive; or the steep climb up
or down through the Wyche Cutting. Those who like a reasonably energetic walk would enjoy going along the whole length of
the hills from north to south, either in easy stages or in a day's
leisurely climb over the various summits.

The quarrying operations which are creating such ugly havoc
on North Hill make it difficult to start at the northern tip of the
hills. I personally find a good way to begin is by the broad track
by the Clock Tower at North Malvern which leads up the flank of
North Hill. This goes up to Ivy Scar Rock, and ever-widening
views over the Severn valley are spread out below like a map.
From here too you can see the extensive building development of
Malvern and Great Malvern; and as a comforting corrective
there is an especially impressive view of the priory church
linking the old with the new. Just before the rugged castellated
Ivy Scar Rock there is a smaller rising path doubling back north-
wards. You turn up here, and, although the ascent is fairly
gradual, it gives you a dizzy sense of exhilarating height above the
land below—almost a sense of dangerous mountainous height for
such little climbing effort.

Soon you arrive at a broad track encircling the eastern side of
the summit of North Hill, past the forbidding dark grey outcrops
of rocks; and once again Great Malvern is spread below you, but
now more clearly. The tower of the priory church seems doubly
impressive from this height, and you can identify buildings far
away, even at this distance, with that odd impression of special
clarity which you have when looking through a telescope. There
is an infinite variety of light and shade over the Severn valley,
changing continually at various times of the day and at different
times of the year; and from here you have a special appreciation of
the way Malvern buildings cling to the steep hillside, for suddenly
you realize that you are looking not *at* chimney-pots, but *down*
them. It is fascinating too, to hear how sounds rise with surprising clarity, and to experience the sense of detachment which
such far-off sounds can bring. The barking of a dog, the sudden
burst of traffic noise or the *staccato* rattle of a pneumatic drill, all
seem curiously unreal at this height.

Worcestershire Beacon rises sharply ahead, criss-crossed by
numerous winding paths, and the squat direction indicator on the
summit stands out clearly against the skyline. On the right is the
miniature peak of Sugar Loaf Hill, and on the left are the creased
folds of valleys covered with bracken or dark with trees. St Ann's
Well can be clearly seen with its shorter, more direct path to the
Beacon from Great Malvern itself. The Conservators have
obligingly marked out on stone indicators the more important
paths, and I prefer to take that marked to West Malvern to go
over Sugar Loaf Hill, because I never tire of the sudden sight
of the glorious view on the western side, with its rolling billows
of wooded hillocks and the jagged outline of the distant Welsh
mountains. From here a ridgeway path climbs steadily to the
top of the 1,395 feet of the Beacon, the highest point of the
Malverns.

All kinds of claims have been made for the extent of the view
from the Worcestershire Beacon. Experienced local observations
confirm that fifteen counties are almost certainly visible in suitable
atmospheric conditions; and two or three more are more doubt-
fully claimed. The fact is that visibility varies so much from day to
day, and so much even from hour to hour, that distant features
come into view or fade away with equal variability. During
the many times I have stood on the Beacon I have continually

discovered some new hill or new building which I have not seen before; and often I have been unable to locate some landmark which I have found with ease at other times. The direction indicator—or toposcope, to give it the technical name—was set up on the Beacon summit to commemorate the reign of Queen Victoria. It consists of a pillar on a marble base with the inscription 'THE EARTH IS THE LORD'S AND THE FULNESS THEREOF'; and on a bronze plate there is a map of the surrounding country-side with the direction and distance of various features and places around the landscape. The toposcope adds greatly to the interest of the magnificent views, and confirms that the general range of visibility is roughly from the Wrekin in the north to the Mendip Hills in the south; and from Plynlimmon in the west to Bardon Hill, Leicester, in the east. The view also embraces the three cathedrals of Gloucester, Hereford and Worcester; the six former abbeys or priories of Deerhurst, Evesham, Pershore, Tewkesbury, Great and Little Malvern; and six great battlefields of English history—Edgehill, Evesham, Mortimer's Cross, Shrewsbury, Tewkesbury and Worcester.

As its name implies, this hill was once an important link when danger signals were sent by means of beacon fires. In his *Armada* Macaulay has included it in his description of the great chain of fires which flared up all over England as a warning that the long-awaited Spanish fleet had at last started on its ill-fated attempt to invade this country:

> All night from tower to tower they sprang, they sprang from hill to hill;
> Till the proud peak unfurled the flag o'er Darwin's rocky dales,
> Till like volcanoes flared to heaven the stormy hill of Wales,
> Till twelve fair counties saw the blaze on Malvern's lonely height. . . .

Some three hundred years after the excitement of that July in 1588, a number of Malvern gentlemen determined to test the reliability of the poet's assertion that *twelve* counties could have seen this warning blaze. Casting about for a suitable occasion which could be celebrated in a dignified way, and at the same time provide the means of a practical experiment, they chose the opening of the Malvern Gasworks as a propitious event to mark

with a monster bonfire, and their attempts to assess Macaulay's
accuracy have been described by a contemporary:

> An ample subscription was opened and there was a willing
> committee of assistants. Public attention was generally called
> by the newspapers of the day, and the greatest curiosity as to
> the success of the experiment was excited, not only in
> Worcestershire, but also in the adjoining counties. On the
> arrival of the appointed hour one savant, more enthusiastic
> in the cause, or more adventurous than his fellows, had
> chosen the top of Snowdon for his observatory whence he
> saw, or probably fancied he saw, the looked-for illumination.
> On many other distant or nearer eminences whence it was
> thought possible or probable that the expected lighting-up
> could or would be visible, stood eager gazers, led thither by
> curiosity or love of science, but all alike more or less doomed
> to disappointment.
>
> Loaded wagons containing coals, wood, tar barrels and
> other combustibles were hauled up by strong teams of
> horses to the summit by a new road first made accessible to
> such conveyances. Materials had been duly but unskilfully
> heaped together by the ready hands of strong-armed stokers,
> more zealous than discreet; and forty torch-bearers, followed
> by many a shouting flambeau-carrying satellite, had started
> from their rendezvous at Saint Ann's Well. Disregarding a
> stormy and tempestuous night they marched upwards in
> martial rank and surmounted the zig-zag path to kindle the
> pile. Alas, alas, the huge pile spreading abroad little else than
> dense volumes of murky smoke obdurately refused to burst
> out as wished into clear bright blaze. A greater failure could
> hardly have resulted, and an interesting problem still
> remains to be solved.

In a recent number of *Country Life*, Alban Claughton, a former
organist of the priory church, has written an amusing account of
another memorable excursion to the top of Worcestershire
Beacon. This was in 1901, when the toposcope was officially
unveiled by the senior members of the local council. The vicar of
the priory church decided that there ought also to be some sort of
religious service at the ceremony, and he arranged that clergy and
choir should process to the summit of the Beacon, and sing a
hymn so that the indicator should be dedicated to the greater
glory of God.

In due course [says Mr Claughton] on a fine day with a slight breeze, we assembled in the big choir vestry of the Priory Church in the early afternoon. Some local clergy had been invited to attend, and we were all robed, the choir, boys and men, in cassocks and surplices. We started out from the church—the choir leading. When the members of the choir were all outside, I noticed to my horror that the men had put on every kind of headgear common to the period. There were trilbys, straw boaters, a bowler and a variety of cloth caps. The effect of it on top of surplices and cassocks had to be seen to be believed.

I hurriedly consulted with one of our clergy, and between us we persuaded the men (and it took some persuasion) to leave this quite unsuitable top-dressing in the vestry. In spite of a few forcibly-expressed anxieties as to catching deaths from cold, the procession started off again in good order.

As we crossed the main road at the top of the town, we must have caused some astonishment. Nothing like this was likely to have been seen since the old monks made pilgrimages, as no doubt they did, to the sacred well of Saint Ann—about half way up the hill. We soon left the main road and started up the steep and narrow route leading to the heights.

When they arrived at the summit and gathered round the indicator it was discovered that although the harmonium had been carried up to this breezy height they had forgotten to bring the seat; and an attempt to try the instrument without the help of a seat resulted in the whole of its inside falling out on to the ground.

At that devastating moment it occurred to me that my guardian angel had foreseen trouble from the start, because something had prompted me to put a pitch-pipe in my pocket—one of those little brass pipes that, on being blown, produce a couple of notes; you inhale for one note and exhale for the other. Luckily the choir knew the music of the *Benedicite* very well indeed, and after I had given them the requisite starting note they got through it unaccompanied with great success.

After this, the chairman of the council made a little speech, unveiled the indicator and declared it open to the public. The vicar duly pronounced the blessing of the Church, a very well-known hymn was sung, and the official proceedings were over. Then, as a final revenge for having failed to wreck the show, Fate played her last card, and down came the rain. Instead of forming up for a dignified return journey, all the members of the choir ripped off their surplices and cassocks, tucked them under their arms and rushed in a most disorderly and undignified fashion down the steep hillside to the comparative shelter of the well.

The toposcope may have been duly blessed and opened, but unfortunately it was not properly orientated. It was later discovered that the directions on the bronze map were off course, and the indicator had to be dismantled and readjusted. But no one, to Mr Claughton's intense relief, ever suggested that the re-sited indicator needed re-blessing.

One of the special attractions of the toposcope is that it provides an incontestably valid excuse for a halt, and it can be examined for just that length of time needed for the least energetic climber to recover breath without losing face. A less subtle but equally understandable opportunity for a halt is provided by the Beacon Café, discreetly hidden in a fold of the summit and open during the season.

The southerly path from the Beacon keeps closely to the undulations of the ridge, and the wide expanse on both sides give an opportunity of trying to decide whether east or west provides the finer view. I find it an impossible decision to make, except perhaps at sunrise and sunset. To see the dawn break and gradually flood the Severn plain is an unforgettable experience; and sunset is equally impressive when the evening sun sinks down with fiery clouds behind the fierce black outlines of the far-off mountains of Wales, and the shadow of the hills creeps along the broad vale of Severn, slowly climbing the slopes of Bredon Hill until the last reflected glow fades away in the gathering darkness. On the western side there still remains some colour from the hidden sun—a sullen purple, and then a greyish mauve with a hint of green in the clearer sky above, until here too night falls at last and stars begin to show.

When the hills reach the Wyche, the path sinks down to the road and starts again on the other side; but 'sinks down' is only relative, because the road here is still nine hundred feet above sea level, as anyone who has stood here in the teeth of a strong wind will appreciate. The Wyche cutting was made through solid rock during the middle of last century, and transformed what was formerly a rough pass into a busy highway. One look at the old Wyche Road will give the modern traveller a healthy respect for the skill and courage of those intrepid riders and coachmen of former times, and grateful relief for the improvements of modern highways.

Climbing up again on the other side of the road, the ridgeway paths now cross over Perseverance Hill and the Pinnacle. This stretch might almost be regarded as a miniature of the whole range's easier walking, and it can be reached quickly and with little effort by numerous paths on both sides of the hills. All along this section, the least energetic climbing is rewarded by magnificent and characteristic views, not only east and west but also southwards, over the spine of the undulating crest of the hills towards the clearly etched spiralling entrenchments of the Herefordshire Beacon. The choice of paths brings the further advantage of allowing the walker to take the lee side of the crest in an east or west wind.

After about a couple of miles the path once again leaves the hills and joins the roads which meet near Wynd's Point, where the British Camp Hotel lies below the towering mass of the Beacon. In W. S. Symonds's novel *Malvern Chase*, set in the period of the Wars of the Roses, there is a mention of 'the little hostelry by that road below the great British Camp near which nestles the ancient Priory of Little Malvern'. Parts of the present hotel [1] have been described as dating back to the fifteenth century, and this suggests that there may well have been an inn beside this once lonely pass of the Malvern Hills during an even earlier period. It is said with more certainty to have been used as a place of refreshment and billeting during the Civil War, especially during the campaign which ended with the 'crowning mercy' of the battle of Worcester.

The now almost forgotten local novel *Malvern Chase* mentioned the 'little hostelry' at Wynd's Point in the course of a description of the journey made by the hero Hildebrande de Brute, when he had the honour of escorting Edward IV's queen and her daughter Elizabeth of York to Malvern Chase while the King was

[1] The British Camp Hotel: apparently it was originally known as Peter Pocket's. *See* Brian S. Smith, *History of Malvern*.

hunting in the district. Hildebrande was at Birtsmorton when he received the royal summons to present himself at Great Malvern.

It was in the year of grace 1482 and about the time of Midsummer, as I was fishing and watching the glimmering chafers in the great fishpool above our moat, that a rider appeared before the drawbridge, charged with a message from King Edward, commanding me to attend him forthwith at Great Malvern, whither he had journeyed accompanied by his Queen, his son the Prince of Wales, and the Princess Elizabeth. I wondered greatly at the King's arriving thus at this lonely village in Malvern Chase. Then the messenger told us that the Queen would have the forest driven for deer for the pleasure of her princely boy, and would try a venture with her own cross-bow.

The sun was rising and bathing the heights of the beacon hills of Worcester and Hereford with golden light as I rode on the gallop by the green glades of Castlemorton towards the Priory of Little Malvern. As I crossed the streamlet which flows from the pass of the Gullet, a bright blue kingfisher shot like an arrow up the waters and a gallant stag arose among the ferns below Wynd's Point and tossed his antlers as if in defiance. Taking the forest ride below the Holy Well I disturbed several hinds and their fawns, but they soon disappeared in the woody dingles along the base of the hills. Arrived at the Priory at Malvern I now learnt why I was summoned to attend the King. Queen Elizabeth wished to ascend the Malvern heights and behold with her own eyes from these lofty crests, the cathedral towers of Gloucester where her royal husband first raised his standard; the city of Hereford, the scene of his revenge for Wakefield; the distant field of Mortimer's Cross; and the hill which rises above Tewkesbury, and round which raged the battle of his crowning glory.

Thus it was arranged that I should attend upon the Queen and the Princess Elizabeth, and guide them to Wynd's Point where palfreys would meet us. While at this pass it was probable that her Majesty might transfix a buck with her own bolt as he passed the borders into the woodlands of Colwall. The Princess insisted upon walking the whole distance to Wynd's Point and soon we reached the Well of Saint Ann which is a hollow in the rock surrounded by ferns and leafy foliage, and into which flows an unceasing streamlet of health-giving waters. Taking the Gullet above the well we ascended slowly listening to the cuckoo's note, and the chiff-chaff of the willow wren, or watching the stone-chats as they perched upon the brambles.

On arriving at the summit of the Worcestershire Beacon the glorious view almost startled the Princess as she stood wondering at the hills of blue in the northern distance. Then we left the bare hill summit and took our way downwards by the pass of the Wych and came to that spot near Wynd's Point where great elm trees rise above a little spring. It is here, tradition says, the visions came to Will Langland which he related in his *Complaint of Piers the Ploughman*; and it was of this water where grow the marsh violet and the woolly grass, that he wrote, 'I was very forwandered and went me to rest under a broad bank by a burnside, and as I lay and looked in the water I slumbered in a sleeping it sweyved so merry.' Arrived at Wynd's Point the merry Princess asked to be conducted to the 'Hermit's Cave' which she had heard of as being at different times the refuge and hiding place of Sir John Oldcastle and Owen Glendower when he had taken refuge in the wilds of Herefordshire.

We now passed on from the little hostelry by that wild hollow below the great British Camp near which nestles the ancient Priory of Little Malvern. No rocks frown here from the mountain's brow, but green grass covers the hill slopes where the coney burrows, and the whinchat lays its blue eggs among the yellow gorse. With the exception of a cowled monk from the monastery, an occasional traveller from the hostelry, one may go for days without meeting a human being in these solitudes. With wild forests all around, the camp above, once occupied by an armed multitude, is now a waste, the haunt of the eagle and the kite, save when some antlered stag seeks its solitude. Now its great trenches and deserted vallum are sole memorials of the past, where British bards and Roman legions have in turn looked forth on the surrounding regions, and beheld the Cotswolds on one horizon and the mountains of Wales on the other. Taking our route below the camp we soon reached the Hermit's Cave above the well of Walm.[1]

The steep path leading to the summit of the Beacon is on the other side of the road opposite the hotel. A stone tablet has

[1] The quotation has been slightly abbreviated.

an inscription which is read by thousands of visitors during the year:

HEREFORDSHIRE BEACON. HEIGHT 1,115 FEET.

One of the finest earthworks in Britain; built about the second century B.C. later enlarged and altered before the Roman Conquest. It dominates the vicinity and commands magnificent panoramic views esteemed by John Evelyn the diarist to be one of the goodliest vistas in England.

The Red Earl's Dyke running along the crest of the hills was made by Gilbert de Clare, Earl of Gloucester, circa 1287 to mark the boundary between his territory and that of the Bishop of Hereford.

At a spring nearby William Langland the famous fourteenth century poet 'slombered in a sleping' and dreamt his 'Vision of Piers Plowman'.

The camp is certainly an impressive stronghold, with a circumference of a mile and three-quarters and an area of nearly forty-five acres. Its great entrenchments, still remarkably well preserved, vary in depth from six to twelve feet, and in places they are thirty feet across. The concentric lines of ramparts circle upwards to the camp citadel, which is about fifty yards across and is defended by a thick stone wall and a deep 'last ditch'. The hill is in any case a magnificently steep natural fortress, and these fortifications must have made it almost impregnable in ancient times, especially as it has been estimated that it could give cover and attacking advantage for as many as twenty thousand men. Its importance was enhanced by its position overlooking the only pass which then existed through the Malvern Hills, and the extent and strength of these steep ramparts and deep fosses, and the cunning disposition of the camp's entrances, all show that it must have been manned as a permanent fort, and not just as a place of emergency defence.

The origins of this great hill fortress must stretch back into the mists of prehistory, and the Britons and Romans who used it must have strengthened, elaborated and added to fortifications which were already ancient. Traditionally this is the site of one of the last stands of the British chief Caractacus against the relentless advance of the Roman legionaries towards Wales. For most of us the important date of the Roman invasion is 55 B.C., and we are inclined to forget that Julius Caesar's landings in that year and in the following year were merely punitive expeditions. Not until close on one hundred years later was there a real invasion under the general Aulus Plautius with the avowed object of subduing the country. His successor, Ostorius Scapula, sought to push the conquest further, and carry the Roman arms beyond the Severn. To do this he had to crush brave dogged resistance from Britons fighting under the inspired leadership of Caractacus, who, according to tradition, had entrenched his forces in this great stronghold on the Herefordshire Beacon. Here they held out for some time, and were only defeated after much sombre bloody fighting.

To complete the story we may add that the final subjugation of Caractacus traditionally took place at Caer Caradoc beside another hill camp between the rivers Teme and Clun. He fled north and took refuge among the Brigantes, whose queen, Cartimandua, ignobly betrayed him to the Romans. It is pleasant to recall that the Emperor Claudius was so moved by his dignified, manly bearing when he appeared in chains before him that he gave him his freedom and restored him to his family.

I have known the British Camp in all seasons and in all weathers, and even when its car park is full, and a milling crowd of happy climbers swarm over its footpaths, it never wholly loses its stark beauty and its inscrutable melancholy. When it is deserted, at dawn or at sundown, or when clouds descend on the hills and there is a strange expectant hush in the mist, the hill has a special atmosphere of uneasy apprehension, reminding us that this is haunted ground peopled by the ghosts of those who perished in those battles of long ago. It is an atmosphere which has been so subtly recaptured by the late Poet Laureate John Masefield in his poem *On Malvern Hill*:

> There by the gusty coppice border
>   The shrilling trumpets broke the halt,
> The Roman line, the Roman order,
>   Swayed forwards to the blind assault.
>
> Spearman and charioteer and bowman
>   Charged and were scattered into spray,
> Savage and taciturn the Roman
>   Hewed upwards in the Roman way.

> There—in the twilight—where the cattle
>   Are lowing home across the fields,
> The beaten warriors left the battle
>   Dead on the clansmen's wicker shields.
>
> The leaves whirl in the wind's riot
>   Beneath the Beacon's jutting spur,
> Quiet are clan and chief, and quiet
>   Centurion and signifer.

The Herefordshire Beacon also figures in John Masefield's enchanting fragment of biography, *Grace Before Ploughing*. He describes a visit to the hill as a small child. He was driven there from Ledbury, and when they arrived at Wynd's Point he was helped down and allowed to climb up the face of the Beacon just below the first great trench, while the others came up the usual way. It was his first walk by himself on any Malvern hill, and with all the sensitivity of childhood he sensed the brooding mystery of this ancient place. The silence of the trench he slithered into was broken only by the strange noise of the wind, and made it a place 'too lonesome and uncanny' to linger in; and he was glad to rejoin the rest of the party.

> After this, we walked down the hill, taking a look at some of the trenches, which gave me the feeling that they have never failed to give me, of vastness, of roughness, and of something vast, rough and uncanny with a life of its own, like itself everlasting and strange; not inhuman, but not human.
>
> I have that sense of it still, and marvel at it. The rough wild hill is impressed with a rough wild life that is strangely greater than anything alive now.
>
> I have no recollection of the return journey to Ledbury; possibly I was asleep before we reached home. I felt, later, that I had been in some way linked with the Herefordshire Beacon; I have that feeling still; and that somehow it is too great for the men of this time to interpret.
>
> People there had made the earth their father and protection; and the earth remembered that, and they, as parts of the memory of the earth, could still impress and terrify. Often they have terrified me.

To read such poetry and such prose inspired by the Hereford-shire Beacon makes us regret all the more the banal words which were set to the music of Elgar's *Caractacus*; as Basil Maine has suggested: 'If Masefield had been the librettist, *Caractacus* might well have been Elgar's opera.'

The Malvern Waterworks reservoir east of the Beacon, below Tinker's Hill, was made over seventy years ago. Although a wall had to be built on one side, the lower slopes of the Beacon itself form the setting of the other three sides, so that the small lake fits in surprisingly well with its surroundings, and even has an interest of its own, especially when it is ruffled by the wind and reflects the changing colours of light and cloud effects. Little Malvern Priory also makes a pleasing picture from this high vantage point, and looks oddly foreign with its pyramidally roofed tower and its truncated nave. On the western side the grey battlements of Eastnor Castle stand out boldly, and at this distance seem like the backcloth of some fairy play. Nearer, against the sky-line to the south-west, stands the tall finger of the Eastnor obelisk.

The name 'Giant's Cave' on the stone direction block must bring a good many people along this path in the hope of seeing a cavern of impressive proportions, but Clutter's Cave, as it is more properly called, turns out to be a modest cavity hewn out of a spur of rock, not more than six feet high and six feet wide inside, and some ten feet in depth. Such a cave could hardly have sheltered a giant, but it is none the less something of a mystery. It seems obviously made by man, but when, and for what purpose? Did it originally shelter shepherds, or some hermit; and has the tradition linking it with the fugitive John Oldcastle and Owen Glendower any basis in fact? And if Clutter was a person, who was he, and why was it his cave? There is no record of any kind of answer to any of these questions, but certainly the cave would have made an ideal shelter for hermit or herdsman, especially as it is so conveniently close to the spring of Walm's Well.

Passing the hump of Hangman's Hill on the left, the path leads on to Pink Cottage. It is no small advantage to have the obelisk before you as you walk: it is a comforting indicator of your progress as it steadily grows larger and clearer. It is also an extraordinarily sensitive reflector of light and shade in the vagaries of English weather, and I never cease to be surprised how rapidly its column can change from staring white to sullen dark grey, with all the subtle gradations of shades between the extremes.

At Pink Cottage the Severn plain east of the hills comes into view again, and spread out immediately below are the flat stretches of Castlemorton Common dotted with grazing sheep looking at this distance like toyland models. The way continues up the small bare shoulder of Swinyard's Hill, a corruption of Swineherd's Hill, for here in the days of the ancient Malvern Forest or Chase, herdsmen with Hanley Castle's permission could drive their animals for summer-time feeding.

The map shows that more quarrying lies ahead, eating remorselessly into the beauty of the hills, and the Conservators have thoughtfully provided another stone direction block, warning the walker to turn right and skirt the Gullet hollow in order to reach Midsummer Hill, and to make the very worth-while detour to the obelisk. The path is along a deeply rutted lane overhung with trees, and this is one of the few places in the walk from north to south along the Malverns where the going can be wet and even muddy at certain times of the year. I have also known it oppressively stifling during a hot summer day, but it is alive with the songs of birds at spring time, and is particularly appealing in autumn with the coloured leaves dropping silently about you as you walk.

By now the obelisk is out of sight, but you find the gate leading to it just before the rise of Midsummer Hill. When you finally reach the crest of the outlying shelf on which it stands, the first feeling perhaps is one of disappointment that it seems rather lower than its ninety feet. It is in fact dwarfed by the magnificence of its situation, but this of course is in itself a tribute to the wisdom and skill in choosing a site which gives the column such well-proportioned size and dignity against the horizon. It was built in 1812 as a memorial to members of the Somers family, and a notice reminds the public who come here that 'this obelisk is a memorial to the dead and should be respected as such'; but of course even this plea has not prevented the senseless scribbles which customarily deface monuments of every kind.

The famous member of the family who comes first in order of dates is commemorated on the western panel with the inscription:

> To the memory of John Lord Somers, Baron of Evesham, Lord High Chancellor of England in the reign of William III, and President of the Council in that of Queen Anne,— To the uniform ability and integrity of his public conduct, posterity has done justice by acknowledging, in the most

ample manner, the wisdom of his counsels, and continually appealing both in and out of Parliament, to the opinion of Lord Somers, as the standard of political rectitude. His spirited defence of the seven bishops in a court of justice, and his able speech in Parliament proving the abdication of King James, are well known. The nation, it is generally admitted, is indebted to him above any other statesman for the union between England and Scotland, and the establishment of the Protestant succession. When his political enemies of the day impeached him before his peers, the House of Commons did not appear at the bar of the House of Lords, or attempt to prove a criminal act against him. He was loyal and faithful to the Sovereign whom he served, a sincere and useful friend to his country, and to his family he bequeathed what they ought to value above earthly possessions or dignities—a great and good example; in gratitude for which and in general admiration of his character, this Obelisk is erected by his heir and representative, John Somers, Lord Somers, Baron of Evesham.

The Lord Chancellor died a bachelor, and the inscription on the east side traces the family's inheritance, and explains the re-creation of the title in 1784. The south side remembers the Lord Chancellor's nephew, James Cocks, who

possessed of an ample patrimony, preferred honour to security, and before he had attained the age of twenty, fighting for his country, fell in battle at St. Cast on the coast of France, A.D. 1758.

Ensign James Cocks must have been one of the early victims of a new strategy against the French which Pitt adopted when he joined the government and infused new energy into the prosecution of the Seven Years' War. A series of raids were made on the French coastline with the object of keeping the enemy in a continual state of alarm, thus immobilizing a large number of their troops for defence at home. These scattered attacks in fact inflicted little other damage to the French, and they often proved costly in British lives. Across the Channel in the town of St Cast itself, another stone memorial provides the French version of this bitter and pointless warfare. The monument commemorates a resounding French victory in 1758, when the English invading force had failed in an attack on the neighbouring town of St

Malo. They were making their way back to their fleet of ships anchored in St Cast Bay, and were in turn attacked by a force of French soldiers under the Governor of Brittany, and lost over two thousand men killed or drowned, including Ensign Cocks.

On the north side another inscription records the personal family loss of the Lord Somers who built the memorial. During the Peninsular War the Duke of Wellington made a series of attacks on the fort at Burgos in 1812. They were all unsuccessful, and after a month Wellington had lost two thousand men. He decided to abandon the siege; but it was too late to save the life of Lord Somers's eldest son, Edward Charles Cocks:

> With strong inducements to apply himself to the safer duties of civil life, the energies of his mind determined him on a military career. Having chosen a profession, he devoted himself to it with successful ardour and perseverance; at the age of 26 he fell, respected, beloved and regretted. His great Commander, the Marquis of Wellington, thus officially announced his death to the Secretary of State, Earl Bathurst: 'At three in the morning of the 8th (October, 1812) we had the misfortune to lose the Honourable Major Cocks of the 79th who was Field Officer of the trenches, and was killed in the act of rallying the troops who had been driven in. I have frequently had occasion to draw your Lordship's attention to the conduct of Major Cocks, and in one instance very recently, in the attack of the hornworks of the castle of Burgos, and I consider his loss as one of the greatest importance to this army and his Majesty's service. . . .'
>
> A father who loved and thought highly of his son, feels himself justified in inscribing these truths to his memory; and bound to add that he acted on public and religious principles, and that he was dutiful to his parents, an affectionate brother, a sincere friend and benevolent man.

In the sloping valley south of the obelisk there are a few scanty remains of the medieval Bronsil Castle, once the home of the great Lord Beauchamp, Lord Treasurer to King Henry VI. A strange legend is told about this now vanished border stronghold. When Peter the Hermit was preaching the Crusade, the Lord of Bronsil, an earlier Beauchamp, was fired with religious zeal and set off for the Holy Land. Before leaving home, however, he decided to keep his hoard of gold and silver safe by plunging it into a secret

Realism in mediaeval craftsmanship: Misericords in Malvern Priory church

Little Malvern Priory church and Court

The shadow of Ragged Stone Hill

Hanley Castle village

Longdon
Marsh
in winter

Malvern country westwards

Bromsberrow church

The Malverns from Castlemorton Common

Church Lane, Ledbury

The old School House at Cradley

Birchwood Lodge in 1900

part of the moat around his castle, and a tame raven of his was set to watch over it. The knight consoled his wife by assuring her that if he fell in battle the treasure could be easily found and recovered, provided that all his bones had a Christian burial. Alas, the knight was killed outside Jerusalem, and although his remains were brought back to Bronsil, the fact that the treasure was never found proves that some of his bones must have been mislaid in transit. But it is said that at midnight the hoarse croak of a raven can still sometimes be heard near the site of Bronsil moat, although 'the knight's escutcheon has long since mouldered from the walls of his castle; his castle itself is but a green mound and a shattered ruin; the place that knew him knows him no more; many a race has died since his; and but for the legendary tale, his name itself would be forgotten in the very land which he once occupied with all the authority of feudal proprietor and feudal lord'.

To stand beside this lonely obelisk, and to look down over the site of that ancient castle, always gives me a special 'sense of a conscious past', and of links with 'old, unhappy, far-off things'. It is a mood which John Masefield has so well expressed in his poem *Eastnor Knoll*:

> Silent are the woods, and the dim green boughs are
> Hushed in the twilight: yonder, in the path through
> The apple orchard, is a tired plough-boy
> Calling the cows home.
>
> A bright white star blinks, the pale moon rounds, but
> Still the red, lurid wreckage of the sunset
> Smoulders in smoky fire, and burns on
> The misty hill-tops.
>
> Ghostly it grows, and darker, the burning
> Fades into smoke, and now the gusty oaks are
> A silent army of phantoms thronging
> A land of shadows.

To continue the walk southwards over the hills we retrace our steps towards the Gullet and follow the grassy track up the shoulder of Midsummer Hill. The summit, like that of the neighbouring Ragged Stone Hill, consists of a double peak, one to the west and the other to the east, with a valley open to the south running up between. In addition to the line of the Red Earl's Dyke the remains of a somewhat curiously shaped prehistoric fort can also be clearly seen. The twin peaks are encircled by the usual ditch, and in addition there is a series of semicircular earthworks stretching across the intervening hollow, showing dozens of rounded marks where prehistoric huts once stood. I have often wondered if they were more effective shelters than the rough stone hut which stands on the hill today. Many times during a sudden storm of rain I have optimistically crouched inside it, but invariably I have been driven out again, preferring to face the certainty of steady rainfall rather than the vagaries of sudden drenching spurts from its leaking roof.

When I arrive at the hut I always prefer to make my way to the main Tewkesbury to Ledbury road by scrambling down the path through the trees passing between the two peaks, west of the quarries by the roadside. At the main road turn right and continue for a few yards to the first gate on the left, and leave the broad path from it almost at once, and strike up the slope of the hill; otherwise you will merely walk around the foot of the hill. Looking back as you climb you can see from here the Eastnor obelisk standing out even more bleakly against the skyline, and below you is the monstrous gash of the quarries. The way up to the summit of Ragged Stone Hill is through tall bracken, and it is set about with ash trees, and rowans gay with scarlet berries in autumn time. You arrive on the higher of the twin peaks of the hill—both of them with small outcrops of the dark rock which give the hill its name.

Seen at a distance almost at any point on the west, Ragged Stone Hill often has something of a sinister, almost menacing, appearance; and its bare rugged summit is an equally fitting scene for a haunted hill, and for the story which lies behind the curse of the Ragged Stone's shadow. *The Shadow of the Ragged Stone* is the title of a little-known nineteenth-century novel by Charles F. Grindrod, which is written around the tragic history of the young monk of Little Malvern Priory who in defiance of his vow of chastity fell hopelessly in love. As a punishment he was condemned to the torturing penance of crawling once a day on hands and knees up to the top of Ragged Stone Hill. One day he could bear it no longer, and in his agony of shame and remorse he cursed the hill and all those on whom the notorious shadow of the hill should fall. The novel opens with a short prologue:

The Ragged Stone is a strange-looking, double peaked hill at the southern end of the Malvern Range, and a weird legend clings to it. This legend sets forth that the doom of death or disaster attends whomsoever the shadow falls upon, and there is evidence to show that at certain times a very peculiar shadow (more resembling a heavy cloud) *does* fall, though Science gives a different explanation of the phenomenon from that favoured by the believers, if any such remain, in the legend. The latter, be its interpretation what it might, had long excited in me an interest which grew to be enthralling; and I had somehow, I scarce know why, come to associate it with that other tragical episode belonging to the same county, which readers of history will remember to have been a moving spring in the great quarrel between the famous Thomas à Becket and the First Plantagenet. It was not until a short time ago, however, and after years of vain searching, that I came upon a solution of the enigma.

One late Autumn day, after a long walk, I had been smoking my pipe in the little village inn of Birtsmorton— the place more particularly said to be haunted by the Shadow —and, according to my wont, plying with questions on my favourite subject a couple of plain countrymen who presently, I suppose to escape my persecution, betook themselves to the road outside. It was at this juncture that my only other companion now left in the room, a gentleman who had all this while been quietly seated in the window-sconce without uttering a word, suddenly came to my help, and with results I had little reckoned on. Seemingly struck by my unusual interest in the matter, this gentleman, whose name I presently learned was Aldrich, at once entered with me upon the topic I had broached, and in the course of a long conversation which followed, informed me that he was the direct descendant of the hero of the legend, the latter having been a monk of the Benedictine Priory of Little Malvern, an establishment situated scarce more than a mile from the weird hill itself. . . .

As for the *appearance* itself, my companion had only once seen it, on the occasion preceding his father's death, and he described it to me as a black columnar cloud which rose up from between the two peaks of the hill, hanging over the scared gazers, and slowly following them as they walked back home, until they had reached the very gate of their house; but to his wife and child it had, or they had fancied that it had, assumed a more definite shape, resembling, they declared, a cowled monk; and the little boy in particular had cried out on first seeing it that it was 'just like the monk's figure in the picture-book'.

In front of you lies the end of the walk—Chase End Hill with the small dark lump of its Ordnance Survey Triangulation Station showing up against the sky. From Ragged Stone Hill you drop down into a little valley with the picturesque name of Whiteleaved Oak. A small cluster of cottages are sprinkled over this secluded pass across the hills, and at one point in the valley here the three counties of Worcestershire, Herefordshire and Gloucestershire all meet. The climb up the slope of Chase End Hill is steep, but at last you stand by the Ordnance Survey's concrete block at the southern tip of the Malvern Hills, having walked some ten miles from North Hill if you take into account climbing up and down the slopes. Standing here you are rewarded by a last magnificent view from the hills, a view which gives you the heady sensation of being on the prow of a great ship thrusting its way forward into the wide green heaving sweep of the country-side spread all around it.

This is historic ground, the southern end of the ancient Malvern Chase and the limit of the medieval boundary set up by the Red Earl between his hunting territory and that of the Bishop of Hereford. It is land which must be peopled by the ghosts of the past—marching troops, gay cavalcades of hunting parties with proud lords and graceful ladies, and sober-clad monks who, half disapprovingly, half regretfully, watch them pass into a romantic golden distance, while they return once more to the hushed peace of prayer and meditation in the cloistered calm of their Malvern priories.

CHAPTER SEVEN

Around the Eastern Slopes

THIS chapter describes the Malvern country which lies to the east of the hills, starting from the north where the approach from Worcester gives a fine view of their sudden purple outline; and where mercifully at this point the hideous gash of the quarries on North Hill is not quite so obvious; although it shows sufficiently to make us regret the wicked destruction which quarrying has made and still makes on these hills.

The village of Newland lies just on the edge of the main Worcester to Malvern road, but on its pleasant triangular village green, shaded by high trees, the clatter of the nearby traffic is surprisingly muffled. Newland once had an interesting timber-framed church dating back to the reign of Edward the Third, but the rebuilding zeal of the nineteenth century swept this away, with the exception of its chancel which was rebuilt in the church-yard to the south of the old site, where it can still be seen with its original window framed in wooden tracery obviously carved out of one single piece of oak—a splendid example of ancient crafts-manship. The original Norman font with a strongly marked criss-cross border around its stem has also been preserved in the new church.

It is impossible not to deplore the disappearance of such an interesting old church, but the present one, built in 1864, makes an impressive outline from the outside with the almshouses attached to it facing an idyllically peaceful setting of trees and lawns at the rear. These almshouses are undeniably handsome, with their imposing gateway and tower and lofty, twisted, Tudor-styled chimneys; but the overall effect on the north side has been sadly spoilt by the ugly blocks which have been added in front of the gables in order to convert the building into a number of very com-fortable flats, for in these days quite a number of the residents here pay for, or towards, their accommodation, and they are no longer 'twenty-four poor men and women who have been employed in agriculture' for whom the third Lord Beauchamp originally intended this charity.

The greatest surprise of all is inside the church which is covered—literally covered, every square inch of walls and roof, and even the organ—with a remarkable series of paintings in 'spirit fresco'. They represent a bewildering variety of biblical and other Christian subjects, a variety which needs a descriptive list to do it full justice.

NAVE: The *Ceiling* is painted with broken chains to represent St Leonard to whom the church is dedicated. St Leonard, the patron saint of prisoners, is said to have been given permission by the Frankish King Clovis to release any prisoners he visited, and he is usually represented holding a captive's broken chains or fetters in his hands.

NORTH WALL (*Upper*). Miracles.
1. The Miracle of Cana in Galilee.
2. The Miracle of the Loaves and Fishes.
3. The Miracle of the Raising of Lazarus.

(*Lower*). The Corporal Works of Mercy.
1. The Giving of Alms.
2. Feeding the Hungry.
3. Giving Drink to the Thirsty.
4. Clothing the Naked.
5. Taking in Strangers.
6. Visiting the Sick.
7. Consoling the Prisoners.
8. Burying the Dead.

SOUTH WALL:
(*Upper*). Parables.
1. The Parable of the Good Samaritan.
2. The Parable of the Great Supper.
3. The Parable of the Talents.
4. The Parable of the Pharisee and Publican.

(*Lower*). The Beatitudes.
1. Blessed are the Persecuted (St Stephen).

2. Blessed are the Peacemakers (Queen Esther before King Ahasuerus).
3. Blessed are the Pure in Heart (The Annunciation).
4. Blessed are the Merciful (Pharaoh's Daughter and the Infant Moses).
5. Blessed are They who Hunger and Thirst after Righteousness (Martha and Mary).
6. Blessed are the Meek (Jacob before Esau).
7. Blessed are They that Mourn (Mary Magdalene).
8. Blessed are the Poor in Spirit (David in the sheepfold).

WEST WALL

(*Upper*) The Pool of Bethesda. The 'healing leaves' (Rev. xxii. 2).

(*Left Oriel window*) St Leonard and St James.

(*Right Oriel window*) Christ as the Bridegroom with the Wise Virgins on his right, and on his left the Foolish Virgins.

(*Oriel window, below*) The Sick Man let down through the Roof (St Luke v.).

CHANCEL

(*Ceiling*) Elements of Water, Earth and Air.

(*Chancel Arch*) The Judgment, with Eve on the left and the Virgin Mary on the right.

(*North wall, upper*) The Triumphant Entry into Jerusalem.

(*North wall, lower*) The Virgin Martyrs—Dorothea, Margaret, Agnes, Katherine, Barbara, Etheldreda.

(*South wall*) The Visit of the Magi. The Nativity.

EAST END

(*North wall, left*) The Resurrection.

(*North wall, right*) The Ascension.

THE CREDENCE

Melchisedec and Aaron.

CHANCEL AISLE

(*Arches*) Six Doctors of the Church—Gregory, Augustine, Ambrose, Athanasius, Basil, Chrysostom.

(*Over the Arches*) The Vine, and the Figures of our Lord.

(*South wall*) Sarah, Rebekah, Rachel, Ruth, the Virgin Mary, Salome, Joanna, Susanna.

(*West wall*) Dorcas, Priscilla, Phoebe, Lois, Lydia.

THE ORGAN
Asaph, Ethan, St Christopher (Ps. cl).

OUTSIDE THE SACRISTY
Heman, Eli, Samuel, Hannah.

These paintings, the wealth of stained glass, the coloured marble pillars, the elaborately carved altar-piece and the encaustic tiles give an impression of almost oriental extravagance in the richly dim religious light of the church. Some may think it rather too much of a good thing, but it is certainly unforgettable, and in any case the church is also worth a visit to see the elaborate oriel window which juts into the building through the west wall, and which was made so that sick members of the almshouse in former days could follow the service without having to make their way into the church. This interesting device had its counterpart in monastic times when aged and infirm monks were able to witness the celebration of the Mass through a similar window or projecting gallery.

You leave Newland for Madresfield by a shady lane with a view of the Malverns stretching into the distance on the right, and showing an occasional glimpse of the priory church against the background of the Worcestershire Beacon. A signpost, 'Callow End', *en route* recalls the time when this was forest land and charcoal-burning country, for names like 'Callow End', 'Picken End', 'Russell's End', 'Drugger's End', 'Gilbert's End' and 'Piper's End', which can be found in Malvern country, originally referred to the 'end' of a forest path which a particular charcoal-burner claimed as his own territory. There is an attractive black-and-white timbered house on the right of the road before you come to the lodge gates of Madresfield Court which has been the home of the Lygon family for generations. The present house is the result of a succession of additions, replacements and restorations over several centuries, but some original Tudor features remain. This is a private house and it is not open to the public. Mercifully an Englishman's castle is still precariously his home, and so it is unnecessary to describe Madresfield Court in further detail. Those who are addicts of 'stately homes' even when they can be visited only vicariously, so to speak, by means of the printed page, should read the excellent description of this house in Catherine Moody's *The Silhouette of Malvern*.

The church at Madresfield is yet another example of nineteenth-century rebuilding zeal. The original church was a Norman building nearer the Court, and it was replaced in 1852 by a new church built apparently without proper foundations—a striking proof that building standards were not always so much better in those days than some of them are today. After some ten years or so the church showed signs of collapsing, and it was demolished. The present one was built on a new site—a rather sombre building without much interest apart from its handsomely embattled tower with pinnacles which certainly do the architect great credit. In the churchyard is a canopied well, once an attractive gesture to a past age, but now badly rusted. Once there was also a charming lead figure above the grave of a young girl, but it is now smashed, leaving only the pathetic remains of a pair of feet and the epitaph: 'And he said, "Who gathered this flower?" Another gardener said, "The Master," so his fellow servant held his peace.' And he might well indeed in the face of such vandalism or neglect.

The way from Madresfield to Hanley Castle goes through small strips of common land, relics of the former Malvern Chase, where wandering cows and sheep can graze reasonably 'safely', together with tethered ponies. Then the main A 440 road is reached, passes Guarlford church and Rhydd Court (now a school) to one of the lodge gates of Severn End where a turning to the right marked 'To the Church' leads to the village.

The entry into Hanley Castle never fails to have the sudden delight of surprise at finding such an unspoilt village so near a busy main road. It has an ideal setting with a miniature village green shaded by a great cedar tree; an attractive village inn with a name, the Three Kings, commemorating the Magi; some picturesque black-and-white timbered houses; and its church benignly overlooking it all. It is perhaps hardly surprising that on one of my recent visits to the village I found no fewer than seven artists all trying to capture on canvas the atmosphere of the place from a variety of jealously chosen vantage points.

And there is antiquity here as well as peace. The grammar school, for example, has a foundation dating back more than six centuries; and the former castle was associated with many figures of history, including the notorious Red Earl of Gloucester who was responsible for the boundary dyke on the Malvern Hills.[1]

[1] *See* page 26.

The great castle with its keep, moat and four towers has virtually disappeared: only a few traces can be seen about a quarter of a mile south of the church. It fell into disrepair towards the end of the fifteenth century, and by the time of James the First it was reduced to 'a great heap of rubbish and a silly barn'. About a hundred years later the last surviving tower was pulled down to provide material for the repair of the old bridge over the Severn at Upton.

In former times Hanley Castle was the headquarters of the administrative centre of the old Malvern Chase—no government department, of course, for it was an old timber-framed farmhouse called Hanley Hall some two miles west of the village which is reputed to have been the official residence of the 'Keeper of the Chase'. The house still has a small room where prisoners were supposed to have been kept while awaiting trial.

The first thing that strikes a stranger about the church at Hanley Castle is the odd position of its tower which stands at the south side, between the nave and the chancel. The present building of stone and brick belongs in part to medieval time and in part to the seventeenth century. The appearance of the inside of the church is spoilt by an ugly wooden door and screen hiding a makeshift vestry, but there are several interesting things to see here. One of my favourites is the cheerfully bright nineteenth-century window on the south side of the west wall which shows, among other things, a lively scene of the Day of Judgment with souls being weighed in the balance. Those passing the test are ushered into heaven with expressions of obvious thankfulness; while those found wanting are haled away in chains to some very realistic-looking flames.

The chapel on the north-east side of the church has a number of memorials to members of the Lechmere family, dating from the sixteenth century. One particularly appealing effigy shows the small kneeling figure of Winifred Lechmere, 'daughter of the Lechmeres of Fanhope'. Another memorial recounts the exploits of a commander in the Royal Navy of the time of Queen Anne.

This is in Memory of Captain Edmund Lechmere formerly Commander of Her Majesty's Ship *Linn* and late of ye *Lime*, frigate of 32 guns on Board of which he departed this Life ye Sixteenth of January 1703 of ye Wounds he received ye Fifteenth in an Engagement with a French Privateer of 46

Guns from which he protected a large FLEET of MER-
CHANT SHIPS all into Safety and then bravely gave ye
Enemy Battel, and forced Him to bear away with very much
Damage. He was in ye Beginning of ye Action wounded in
both knees and afterwards received a Musquet Shot through
his Body yet by neither discouraged from prosecuting ye
Enemy with ye utmost Vigour. Thus fell this brave Man. . . .

A cottage at the bottom of Quay's Lane is the reputed birthplace of another Edmund of a very different character—Edmund
Bonner, the sixteenth-century bishop who was so notorious for
the part he played in the persecutions of Queen Mary's reign.

He was born here at the beginning of the sixteenth century of
humble parents, but he was educated at Oxford, apparently with
the help of Cardinal Wolsey who took an interest in him. It
would greatly add to the local interest of his story if it could be
proved that it was when Wolsey was chaplain to the Nanfans at
Birtsmorton [1] that he first met his young protégé. This is just
possible of course, but hardly probable as Bonner would have
been only a small child at the time. After Wolsey's disgrace and
death, Bonner continued to enjoy the favour of Henry the Eighth,
and he even had the doubtful privilege of being sent to Rome to
press more urgently the King's claims to divorce Katherine of
Aragon. He was later appointed Bishop of London and although,
like the King himself, a rigid defender of Catholic doctrine
against the reformers, he did acknowledge the principle of the
Royal Supremacy during Henry's reign.

When Edward the Sixth came to the throne, however, and the
reforming party set about abolishing the Mass and sweeping
away images and sacred pictures in churches, Bonner made a
stand and refused to take the Oath of Supremacy. He was deprived of his see and confined in prison until the death of the
young King and the accession of Mary. She restored him to the
see of London, and he served her with fanatical zeal in her moves
to restore papal power and secure obedience to the Catholic
reaction by persecution. When the lonely, embittered Mary died,
Bonner once again refused to take the Oath of Supremacy under
the new Queen Elizabeth.

Bonner has often been represented as a callous monster. This is
undoubtedly an exaggeration, but he was certainly hated, so

[1] *See* page 111.

much so that it is said men would point to any fat ugly fellow in the street and shout: 'That is Bonner!' He had aroused such fierce animosity among so many people during the savage persecutions of the previous reign that under Elizabeth he was perhaps fortunate to suffer only another term of imprisonment, which lasted until his death some eleven years later.

Another native of Hanley Castle, who was born almost exactly a century after Bishop Bonner's death, became notorious for religious views of a much more unorthodox kind. John Asgill was a strange character who gained a great deal of notoriety by publishing an eccentric pamphlet to prove that 'death was not obligatory upon Christians'. He was immediately accused of blasphemy and was duly expelled from the Irish Parliament where he sat as a member. Later he became a member of the English House of Commons, but after a committee had examined the implications of his doctrine he lost his seat there. Asgill was a barrister, and based the arguments of his extraordinary pamphlet on what he considered to be the principles of law. He maintained that 'since Death was the penalty imposed by Adam's sin, and since Christ had satisfied the law, death could no longer be legally inflicted, and all who claim their rights will be exempt'. Apparently Asgill did claim his rights, and maintained that he would be 'translated' without dying, although to all outward appearances he certainly did die in 1738.

As you approach Upton-upon-Severn by the main road from Hanley Castle you have a very good first sight of the impressive spire of its nineteenth-century church towering gracefully upwards for rather more than 180 feet. You can also see nearer the river the strange octagonal cupola crowning a tower—all that remains of the old parish church which was destroyed during the troubles of the Civil War. Upton is, so to speak, the capital of the country east of the Malverns. It is an ancient place full of history and character. There was a time when it had a considerable river trade, and when its bridge was the only one between Gloucestershire and Worcester. 'There is no bridge on Severne above Glocester', wrote Leland in his *Itinerary*, 'tyll the townlet of Upton . . . whither at high Tydes Severne se doth flow', for in those times the river was tidal as far as Upton. Some of the goods unloaded here were taken by pack-horses over the Malvern Hills to outlying villages on the western side.

With all its picturesque antiquity Upton has mercifully not gone 'quaint' or 'Tudor-Tea-Shoppe' minded; it has too much robust dignity for that, and its bridge is still an important link for road transport with a long history. The original wooden structure was replaced in 1605 by a stone bridge, which played a historic part in the Civil War and was never properly repaired. In 1853 it was destroyed by a flood and was in turn replaced by a four-arched bridge with a swinging section. Finally, this was itself superseded by the present handsome structure in 1940, which was fortunate enough to escape destruction by German bombs during the war.

The historic part which the old stone bridge played in the last stage of the Civil War has been described in some detail in E. M. Lawson's *Records and Traditions of Upton-on-Severn*. When in 1651 Charles the Second marched from Scotland with his army of strangely assorted 'Cavaliers, Prelatists and Puritans' to make his final bid for power, he made for the Faithful City of Worcester. His General Massey meanwhile pushed on to Upton with a force of between four and five hundred cavalry and infantry in order to defend this important crossing of the river against a surprise attack by the Parliamentarians. The bridge was already broken down, with two of its arches in ruins; a guard was set over it and the Royalists seemed to be in a strong strategic position, but they were too certain of their security. Very early on the morning of 28th August, a body of Roundheads under Lambert advanced cautiously towards the town. General Massey and his men were sleeping peacefully, little knowing that their guards, who should have been watching the bridge, were carousing in a nearby tavern, and that over the broken arches of the bridge there still stretched a single plank which should have been removed with the others at nightfall, but which either by accident or treachery had been left there overnight. There was enough roadside grass to deaden the sound of horses' hoofs, and the morning mist lay over the river thick enough to hide the invaders.

As the main force made for a ford downstream eighteen men set out to cross by a shorter but more dangerous way. Springing from their horses they bestrode the narrow plank and edged themselves over the river in this precarious fashion. Having reached the other side they lost no time in gaining shelter; they dashed up the slope to the church and were soon safely inside with doors barricaded and muskets guarding every window.

Meanwhile the Royalists had been roused and began a furious attack on the party inside the church. Through the broken glass and shattered woodwork, besiegers and besieged shot and stabbed at each other, but by now the rest of the invaders were fording the river not one hundred yards away, and every minute fresh combatants poured into the churchyard and streets as troop after troop of Ironsides clattered up Dunn's Lane, and more and more of the Royalists were aroused. It was hand-to-hand, desperate, disorderly fighting, but it was too late for Massey to get his men into any kind of order; it soon became obvious that all hope was lost and the Royalists fled in confusion to Worcester. Massey was the last to leave; his horse had been shot under him; he was wounded in several places, but he continued to fight with a cool courage which even his adversaries acknowledged.

It is not uncommon for visitors seeing Upton for the first time to remark on its 'almost continental' appearance. I know the characteristics which make them say this, but for me Upton has always seemed peculiarly English: in fact the epitome of all that is most pleasant in an English market town lucky enough to be set beside the curving banks of the Severn. Nothing surely could be more English than its sturdy black-and-white half-timbered houses and shops; its gables; its Georgian brick; and its links with the past like the site of the scolds' Ducking Stool in New Street marked by a stone pillar with the inscription:

> This is the site of the Goom Stool Cottages which were built at the end of the fifteenth century and demolished in 1882. Near here was a dirty pool where the ancient cucking or ducking stool stood in which slanderous women were tied and ducked up and down in the water.

Above all there are the Upton inns. I have never in fact counted them, but there is a remarkable number and some of them are of considerable antiquity. One, for example, bears the date 1601. Another is the scene of episodes in *Tom Jones*, when Fielding brought 'our hero and his redeemed lady safe into the famous town of Upton and they went directly to that inn which in their eyes presented the fairest appearance in the street, a house of exceeding good repute'. Many of the inns are attractive buildings, especially the black-and-white timbered Anchor, where the unsuspecting Royalist guards are said to have been caught off guard peacefully drinking when Cromwell's soldiers successfully attacked the town in 1651. Then there is the Bell with its copper sign, clapper and all; and the Talbot with its pleasant façade of arched windows and entrance porch. The Swan and the Star overlook the river; and the White Lion has a dignified pillared porch which is a feature of the High Street. This last inn has associations with the actress Sarah Siddons who once performed there with a troupe of strolling players; and one of its former landlords has the distinction of figuring in what is perhaps the best known of all epitaphs:

> Beneath this stone in hope of Zion
> Doth lie the landlord of the Lion;
> Resigned unto the heavenly will,
> His son keeps on the business still.

In the bar of the White Lion there is an interesting old bill advertising the times of the local Malvern coach:

'The Great Western' will leave the Unicorn Inn, Malvern, every morning (Sunday excepted) at ¼ past 9, and the White Lion, Upton-upon-Severn at ¼ past 10 o'clock through Malvern Wells, Hanley, Longdon to the Railway Station, Gloucester, in time for trains to London, Bristol, Bath, Taunton, Exeter, Plymouth. Van goods will be conveyed by Light Cart.

All that remains of Upton's old church is the fourteenth-century red sandstone tower which still retains the eighteenth-century cupola of the building's restoration after its destruction during the Civil War. At the end of the nineteenth century a new parish church was built at the other end of the town, and the old one was allowed to fall into ruin. This may have been a satisfactory solution of a rebuilding problem, but I personally feel an uneasy pang of conscience when I visit the old tower and tread steps and paths made from cracked tombstones of graves, and presumably torn from the last resting-places of Upton forefathers who hoped for a more dignified memorial.

Some four centuries ago a very strange young parson became rector at the old Upton parish church, and later became well-known as the magician, astrologer and alchemist who was consulted by Queen Elizabeth and many other notable people of her time. John Dee was born in 1527 and studied mathematics and astronomy at Cambridge, where he made a name for himself as a brilliant scholar. He was granted a pension by Edward the Sixth, and appointed to the living of Upton in the last year of the young king's reign. Inevitably with the accession of Mary he was regarded with suspicion and hostility. He was accused of plotting against the Queen's life by means of magical spells, was imprisoned and narrowly escaped execution for treason. Mary's death four years later brought him his release, and he enjoyed great favour under Elizabeth, who not only frequently consulted him but even paid him the honour of visiting him at his house.

The Queen is said to have had lessons in astrology from him, and he began to earn an unenviable reputation for dabbling in black magic. Yet there is no doubt that John Dee was a great scholar (he was Warden of Manchester College for nine years), and it is difficult to reconcile this with the mumbo-jumbo of magic and his preoccupations with signs and portents which he records in his diary. One thing is certain: Dee's powers of divination had their limitations. When, for example, he set off on a prolonged tour to exhibit his magic at various courts abroad he did not appear to foresee that during his absence an angry mob bent on a wizard hunt would break into his house and destroy his books and his laboratory. He was even artless enough to expect a substantial pecuniary reward from his parsimonious Queen for his astrological services, but as she herself cryptically remarked to him: 'Dee, there was never promise made but it was broken or kept.' In her case it was broken; John Dee died in abject poverty.

I have already remarked on the graceful distinction of the nineteenth-century church tower and spire, and this is perhaps the most noteworthy feature of a building which starts with the serious handicap of a particularly unattractive and unshapely stone of a sickly bilious yellow. The interior, however, gives an overall impression of space and dignity, and it contains a few memorials salvaged from the old church. The most imposing is the stone effigy of a fourteenth-century knight grasping his sword; the most humble is a simple painted board extolling the virtues of one Elizabeth Pritchard:

> Patient devoted servant of her God,
> The narrow path this humble woman trod,
> Beheld a jarring world & shunn'd its strife,
> Reproving only by her peaceful life.

The book of Truth she ponder'd line by line,
In memory stor'd its oracles divine;
The holy table by her Saviour spread
Duely she sought, to taste of Angel's bread.
Rich in content with piety her gain;
And still devout when tried by torturing pain,
To Him who gave resigning her calm breath
In meek tranquillity she sunk to death,
And now, life's trial done, her sleeping dust
Awaits the glorious rising of the just.

The parish records of Upton date back to 1546, and make
interesting reading with their quaint details which throw unexpected sidelights on life in past centuries. In his book E. M.
Lawson quotes several examples of the care which, unexpectedly
enough, was taken of the poor of the parish during the eighteenth
century. They were provided with clothes, and the youths were
fitted out and paid for as apprentices. In time of sickness they
were treated with special liberality and received gifts of money,
bread, meat, coals and luxuries like 'drink and sack, white brede,
and a leg of lambe'.

Bleeding was resorted to in most cases of sickness, and the
operation was performed at a cost of 6d. to the parish.
Hannah Niblett, who had a bad leg, was bled three or four
times in a month. Soon after the last bleeding, a parish
meeting was held to consider how much should be paid to a
Mr Browne for 'cutting off the pore woman, her legg'.
The following are a few among the many entries which refer
to the medical treatment and relief of the sick poor:

	s.	d.
For blooding ould Griffin and other necessaries	1	6
Old Brick, being a sick family	1	0
Old Brick, to bury his wife and subsist ye rest of his family	16	0
To Mr Airey, for setting Mary Jaxon's arme	2	6
And for cure of Bishop's boy's legg	10	0
Nessessarys for Old Hazell	2	6
For the woman that wacht with him	1	6

The records also reveal that some poor shiftless families were
obviously a perpetual liability. In 1727, for example, the Lippits
were seldom out of some kind of trouble for long.

They were taken before the 'Justis', or lodged in Worcester Gaol, or distrained upon for rent, or coming to grief in some way or other. Some great calamity, resulting in death or maiming, came upon this unlucky family, as may be gathered from these entries:

	£	s.	d.
Coffin, bell, grave, bread, cheese, for Lippitts' girl		8	0
Paid Doctor Harbert for cutting off Lippitt's arme, and what he applied to him before his arme was cut off	7	10	0
Paid Doctor Harbert for cutting off the boy's leg	5	0	0
To ten weeks' pay to the boy and man	3	3	6
For dyates	1	19	10
Linen cloth, burying the arme and leg, charcoal, bringing the old man and boy to town		5	6
A shin of beef for Lippitt and his boy			6

On the other hand, the poor who were not of the parish, and who tried to establish themselves here, or remain for the time being, received short shrift owing to the rule of the old Poor Law which laid down that anyone born in a parish was chargeable to it for life. Consequently any pregnant woman travelling from one place to another was treated with positive inhumanity; she was liable to be harried out of the town or driven in a cart beyond the parish bounds lest another child should burden the rates. Several entries record payments made to some wretched expectant mother 'to persuade her to get out of the place and go away'.

Along the road to Longdon the view of the Malverns is now no longer framed behind a network of trees, but they are seen standing out rather more starkly against the horizon. About a mile before reaching Longdon it is worth while making a short detour by turning right at a signpost marked Hill End and Castlemorton, and going along the road which gives an excellent view of the gabled, black-and-white half-timbered house called Eastington Court, probably one of the oldest in the county, and certainly dating back to the time of Henry the Seventh, with some additions made at the beginning of this century.

The village of Longdon stands on a gentle rise overlooking the flat country which stretches towards the Malvern Hills. Opposite the church is another fine example of a 'magpie', black-and-white, timber-framed house so typical of this district. The church is a fascinating mixture of styles and dates: of the earlier building only the thirteenth-century tower and spire remain; the rest of the building is eighteenth-century with the addition of a nine-teenth-century chancel. It is a refreshingly clear and bright building which is a tribute to its Italianate style and the later Romanesque additions. One of the best things to be seen in the church is the lively brass portraying a sixteenth-century squire, William Brugge, and his wife Alice. Here they are for us to see after all these centuries, beautifully drawn in lifelike detail—she with her endearing little face veiled by a long head-dress; he a burly figure, bare-headed, with skirt of mail and with spurs, and below them a lion and a dog with its collar. Somehow time stands still when you look at these realistic portraits; they are so clear and fresh that you suddenly realize the meaning of A. L. Rowse's remark: 'History is alive and all around us.'

Kelly's *Directory* of 1940 records that the church then possessed 'a representation of the Crucifixion over the communion table, executed in pyrography by a former curate'. Unfortunately this unusual example of ecclesiastical poker-work has now disappeared; it must have been worth seeing as a curiosity.

The higher road from Longdon to Birtsmorton gives the finest view of the Malverns from the eastern side. The entire length of their range can be seen, and it shows up most impressively at sunset, especially when the sky flames crimson against the serrated outline and then slowly turns to a misty shade of light purple before its final change to a hint of pale green in the dying reflected glow of the hidden sun. To pass from Longdon to Birtsmorton is to go through a country with a very different character from other parts of this district. For here is a moorland plain, with that indefinable brooding atmosphere reminiscent of Somerset's Sedgemoor, but on a smaller scale. Longdon Marsh is a land of flat meadows marked by characteristic lines of willows, and with dykes and reeds to remind us that this is country reclaimed from boggy marshland once regularly flooded by a tidal Severn, and salty with the brine washed down from salt springs of Droitwich. Indeed there was a time when rare marsh plants were found in this locality, but with improved drainage these have become rarer than ever. During the years I have known this road to Birtsmorton, I have always noticed how vividly the seasons are reflected on this moorland stretch. Spring quickens early here with a faint green of the willow trees; and in high summer the noonday sun sheds a breathless drowsy haze of moist and earthy heat over the rushes, willow herb and meadow sweet. In autumn the season is marked by wisps of melancholy mist which settle softly over the moor; and later in the year the boles of the willows stand out bleakly against the sky in the icy stillness of a winter's day.

Looking through the eyes of the hero of his novel *Malvern Chase*, W. S. Symonds has given a vivid impression of what Longdon Moor must have been like in the far-off days of the fifteenth century.

When I was about twenty years of age, John Hastings, our forester and woodman, became my frequent companion and it was my delight to persuade him to accompany me to the moor of Longdon where in autumn time we snared snipes and plover in numbers with horse-hair springes, while he would occasionally kill both wild ducks and wild geese with his cross-bow, or the grey goose shaft from the long-bow. In summer time the moor was dry in large portions, though much covered by the bullrush and the flag, and John could always find a heron for our falcons; while many a bittern have we brought home from the moor before the summer's sun had risen above the spire of Longdon. In the summer days flags and rushes held wild ducks' eggs and plovers, with which my mother loved to make a dainty dish when our friends and neighbours came to dine.

One evening in the mid-spring time Hastings told me he had heard a bittern booming at the moon down among the reeds and willows in the moor; so we were up before the sun, the grey mist still hanging over the vale, I with my cross-bow, and Hastings with his long-bow and sheaf of arrows. The sun rose as we neared the moor, and we heard the boom, boom of the bittern, the quack of the mallard, and the shrill cauk, cauk, of the heron. The moor possessed a character of its own. It was if possible more lonely than the Chase, with its scattered villages and granges, and silent as the grave, save the call of its wild fowl and the croak of the frog. There were mires, tall rushes and sedges filled by a spring-time flood, and boggy places which would engulf a man if he slipped in, and cover him up to the day of doom in black peaty slush.

The focal points of interest in Birtsmorton are its church and the manor house adjoining it. Birtsmorton Court is an interesting example of an ancient semi-fortified grange, and its moat and the foundations of the house remain just as they were planned before the Norman Conquest. The oldest part of the building is the great twelfth-century gateway, surrounded by battlements and formerly approached by a drawbridge, traces of which can still be seen. Inside, the most noteworthy features are the Council Chamber, with its splendid sixteenth-century oak panelling; the Great Hall, with its fine moulded ceiling; and the Banqueting Hall, dating from Elizabethan times. At the time of writing the house is undergoing extensive restoration, and the new owner has not yet decided whether she will open the house to the public when the restoration is completed.

Originally Birtsmorton Court was owned by the Nanfan family, and it was here that the young Wolsey started his career as chaplain to Sir Richard Nanfan, who set him on the road to fame and the perils of high office by introducing him to the court of Henry the Seventh. There is a tradition too that even earlier than this Sir John Oldcastle, leader of the Lollards, hid in this house for a time after escaping from the Tower of London, where he had been imprisoned for his heretical views. He is said to have been smuggled out of Birtsmorton later, under cover of darkness, and he managed to reach Wales, where he evaded his pursuers for nearly four years. At length, however, he was run to earth, taken back to London and burnt at the stake.

An even more dramatic fugitive of English history traditionally took shelter inside this peaceful-looking house. During the bloodthirsty confused fighting of the Wars of the Roses the 'She-wolf of France', Queen Margaret of Anjou, is said to have taken refuge here with her young son, Prince Edward. If she did, these walls must surely have echoed to the restless plotting and planning of this ruthless, fearless woman, who a few years later was to be taken prisoner at the battle of Tewkesbury in 1471, while the nineteen-year-old prince was pursued through 'Bloody Meadow'. He was caught by Sir Robert Crofts and taken to King Edward the Fourth, who haughtily asked the young man 'how he durst so presumtiously enter into his realm with banner displayed? Whereunto the Prince boldly answered, saying: "To recover my father's kingdom, and heritage from his father and grandfather to him, and from him, after him, to me, lineally descended." To this bold speech Edward, without deigning any reply, struck him on the face with his gauntlet and retired, whereupon they fell upon the defenceless captive and stabbed him in several places with their daggers as he vainly cried for mercy.'

Lastly, this historic house has a connection with the nineteenth-century statesman William Huskisson, who was born here. Huskisson is remembered not only for his distinguished political career, but also for the tragedy of his death. He was present at the opening of the first double-track railway—Manchester to Liverpool—in 1830. For some time he had been estranged from his former friend the Duke of Wellington, and seeing him in a coach on the other track Huskisson climbed out of his compartment and walked over to effect a reconciliation. Even as they exchanged greetings the train moved forward, and the agonized Wellington saw Huskisson crushed to death before his eyes—the first victim of a railway engine.

Birtsmorton's church of SS. Peter and Paul was originally dedicated to Saint Thomas of Canterbury, whose very name was anathema to Henry the Eighth. On his accession, therefore, the new dedication was tactfully substituted for that of the 'false traitor' (alias 'the holy martyr') of Henry the Second's reign. The church, and especially its fourteenth-century tower, always strikes me as being particularly neat, almost elegant, for its period. There was much rebuilding and restoring here in the nineteenth century, but the original massive early Norman font still remains, and one curiosity which has been kept is a dainty marble altar of the eighteenth century, now placed near the entrance. The main interest of the church for me, however, is its splendid collection of monuments of which the oldest is an especially fine table-tomb with a huge slab of Purbeck marble, and ten remarkably well-preserved carved stone figures around three of its sides. Two centuries ago these figures were identifiable by labels above them which have now disappeared, but the names have fortunately been recorded. The effigy formerly on the slab has also disappeared, but one suggestion is that this is the tomb of the Sir Richard Nanfan, who employed the young Wolsey in his household at Birtsmorton Court. On the other hand, the matrix of the brass shows that it is more likely to be the tomb of Jane, Lady

Houghton, who married three times, and whose second husband was a Nanfan.

To be much married seemed a characteristic of the distaff side of this family. Catherine, the last of the Nanfans, who died in 1737, took her first husband when she was in her teens and her fourth and last when she was over seventy. Her first husband was Richard Coote, later the Earl of Bellamont, who was appointed Governor of New England in 1695, and who was responsible for the capture of the notorious pirate Captain Kidd. On her husband's death the Countess of Bellamont became the wife of William Caldwell, a distinguished naval officer, who 'after his return from his command of being Rear-Admiral of the Red Squadron in the British Fleet in the Baltic died at Birtsmorton Court the 7th day of October, 1718 Ætas 55 '. He is commemorated by a magnificent memorial on the north wall of the church. It shows not only the full-length reclining figure of the mild-faced sailor himself, but also his ship (probably the *Torbay*, a ship of the line he once commanded) and a fascinating collection of twenty-eight navigational instruments, including log book, quadrant, sounding leads, globe, spyglass, compasses and others too complicated for a landlubber to identify.

Catherine Caldwell's third matrimonial venture was with Edmund Pytt, a Member of Parliament; and her fourth husband was William Bridgen, one-time Lord Mayor of London—altogether a quartet of husbands any wife could be proud of.

From Birtsmorton to Berrow the moorland willows give place once again to hedges and winding leafy lanes. It is difficult to realize that here you are less than a mile away from the busy throbbing traffic of a great motorway. Berrow, in the shadow of a wooded hill, seems hushed in the silence of its surroundings, broken only by the call of wood pigeons and the songs of birds. It has a plain homely church, obviously most lovingly cared for. The tower looks strangely clumsy because of its sturdy (almost aggressively sturdy) square turret. A fine timber porch frames a simple Norman arch, and there is an equally fine Norman font inside, as well as two other features more difficult to explain. Why, firstly, is the western arch of the south arcade so oddly cut into the wall? And what was the original purpose of that very deeply splayed window which is cut through the wall on the north side of the chancel?

Outside the church there is a strange inscription on the north wall near the porch which records that

> Under the stone beneath this tablet lie the remains of Edward Gummary, Elizabeth his wife, and Ann their daughter who were cruelly murdered at the cottage known as the Murder House in the parish of Berrow on the night of May 7th 1780.

Berrow, too, has associations with the Nanfan family. In 1745 a Mrs S. C. Nanfan left a legacy of forty pounds for a sermon to be preached every February in Berrow church. This was a thank-offering for her salvation from what she described obscurely as 'the violent and wicked design of an unnatural enemy'. Because some years before the suitor of a Nanfan had been fatally wounded in a duel at Birtsmorton, it was commonly but erroneously supposed that this later legacy specified a sermon against duelling. In fact it did not, and Susannah Cocks Nanfan's 'unnatural enemy' is as much a mystery as ever it was. I can only add that the Nanfan sermon is still preached today, as it has been for the past two hundred years.

It is obviously pleasanter to avoid the main roads as much as possible, and to reach Castlemorton by doubling back to Birts-morton along a road which passes an attractive half-timbered inn, The Farmer's Arms, which has genuine old beams and flag-stones in its friendly bar. The village of Castlemorton is widely scattered, and surrounded by one of the last remnants of the once extensive Malvern Chase—something like six hundred acres of unenclosed common land dotted with sheep, and stretching right up to the lower slopes of the hills. The site of the former castle which gave the place its name is clearly visible south of the church, opposite the newly built school. Both the north and south door-ways of the church are Norman: one with a lamb, the *Agnus Dei*, above it, the other showing a man's head. Inside the church is the largest and ugliest heating stove I have ever seen, but as a palliative you can see on each side of the window, on the north wall, an unusually large and beautifully carved niche, each with a canopy. It will be noticed that the church seems misshapen because the south aisle projects quite considerably at its north end; and the arcade has three and a half arches, with the half built into the west wall—an unexplained oddity which recalls something similar in Berrow church.

A strange incident which occurred at Castlemorton during the Civil War is recorded by T. R. Nash in his *Collections for a History of Worcestershire*; it gives some idea of the breakdown of law and order during that period. One September day in 1642 Ledbury fair had attracted most of the villagers away from their homes and, taking advantage of this, a party of over a hundred soldiers, some from Gloucester, some from Tewkesbury, stormed into Castlemorton intent on plunder. They were led by a Captain Scriven with a respectable background (his father had been Mayor of Gloucester), who incited them to break into the house of a Mr Rowland Barton. He was 'a man much beloved, and for his hospitality so dear to all sorts of people that if the neighbours had not been at the fair, they would have defended his house for him successfully'. As it was, the soldiers forced open a chest and took at least six hundred pounds and stole besides a quantity of linen, plate and jewellery of great value. They then made off, leaving a trail of destruction behind them. Mrs Barton not only lost her jewels but also suffered the indignity of a ransacked kitchen where they had 'scattered her sweetmeats on the ground, not daring to take of them for fear of poison'. Nash adds that the unfortunate Mr Barton's house was plundered again no less than six times during the troubled times of the Civil War.

The road back to Malvern passes through the common, giving another magnificent view of the Malvern Hills, while the common itself offers colour and character throughout the seasons, particularly in autumn when it has been described as 'a riotous feast of colour; behind are the purple hills and all around are the yellows and reds and browns of the gorse and blazing bracken'. The road passes Welland's clean, bright nineteenth-century church, which was built in this more convenient position to replace the demolished seventeenth-century building at the far end of the parish. This new building is worth visiting if only to see the seventeenth-century font, which was taken from the old church and is now preserved in a glass case at the west end. A font in a glass case sounds an impossibility, but this font is ten inches high, surely the smallest font of that age in the country.

It would be satisfying to record that the remains of the old Welland church are equally well cared for. Unfortunately a visit to the site next to the old vicarage and the adjoining eighteenth-century Court reveals that the old parish graveyard is in a sad state of neglect, with rank grass growing over tombs and overturned headstones—

> . . . sunk in shapeless ruin all,
> And the long grass o'ertops the mouldering wall.

CHAPTER EIGHT

Malvern Country Westwards

THE village of Redmarley D'Abitot makes a good starting point for an exploration of the western side of Malvern country from south to north, the direction which gives the best views on this side of the hills and their wooded slopes and valleys. The name Redmarley dates back to Saxon times, but the qualifying D'Abitot was added by the Norman knight Robert D'Abitot, steward of William the Conqueror's household, who was rewarded by the gift of this manor. The family was still living in the parish at the end of the eighteenth century, an example of the persistence of family ties with a place, which is so common in English local history.

Redmarley is now a very small place, but it is surprising to discover from contemporary documents how many craftsmen lived in the village in the mid nineteenth century—no fewer than eighteen carpenters, fifteen masons, thirteen shoemakers, six tailors and five thatchers. Villages of course were more self-supporting in those days, but even so this does seem an extraordinary number of craftsmen for so small a village. Perhaps in a material sense Redmarley has come down in the world since then, although it is still attractive enough, and surrounded by some unspoilt countryside in spite of its proximity to a main road and a motorway. It is certainly an ancient place, as the timbered Tudor house opposite the church testifies, but in spite of its present air of peaceful tranquillity it has had its share of links with great events in the past.

The nearby Bury Court and park were once part of the secular possessions of the See of London, and when Bishop Bonner was sent to his first imprisonment in the reign of Edward the Sixth, Nicholas Ridley was appointed his successor as Bishop of London, and he nominated his brother-in-law, George Shipside, to manage the property at Redmarley. With the accession of Queen Mary, Ridley inevitably lost his see and Bonner was reinstated. Ridley was later arrested, and with Cranmer and Latimer condemned on a charge of heresy. Shipside hurried to Oxford to be with him at the end, and he must have heard Latimer's immortal words as they were being tied to the stake: 'Be of good comfort, Master Ridley. Play the man; we shall this day light such a candle by God's grace, in England, as I trust shall never be put out.' And when Ridley saw his brother-in-law's anguish as the flames flared up he called out with words equally memorable: 'Farewell, my brother George Shipside, whom I have ever found faithful, trusty and loving, in all states and conditions, and now in the time of my cross, over all others to me most friendly and steadfast, and that which liketh me best over all other things, in God's cause ever hearty.'

By one of those strange anomalies which sometimes occurred even in those grim and vindictive times, George Shipside continued to live on in peace at Redmarley until his death over fifty years after Ridley's tragic end, and in the church behind the organ there is a brass to his memory bearing the words:

All flesh is grasse, wormes meat, and clay and here it hath short time to live,
for proofe whereof both night and day all mortall wights ensamples give,
beneath this stone fast closde in clay doth sleepe the corpse of George Shipside,
wch Christ shall rayse on ye last day and then with Him be glorifide,
whose soule now lives assuredly in heaven with Christ our Saviour,
in perfect peace most joyfully with God's elect for evermore.

(He died on the 31st day of December in the year of our Lord 1609, and in the 84th year of his age. See what thou wilt be.)

Thirty-five years after George Shipside's death Redmarley came more uncomfortably close to national history when the tide of the Civil War rolled right into the peaceful village. At that time the city of Gloucester was held by the Roundheads under General Massey, and two royalist forces, one from Hereford and another from Worcester, set out with the intention of joining up and making a combined attack on Massey's troops. Owing to some confusion in their orders the two royalist forces failed to meet, and the men from Hereford made the attack alone. They were easily repulsed and fell back in disorder to Redmarley, hoping to make a safe retreat, but the Parliamentarians followed them with relentless speed. A battle then took place in the village near the church and the royalists were once again defeated and fled to Ledbury.

It is estimated that something like two to three thousand men must have taken part in this fight, and many must have been wounded and perhaps many more killed than the number buried here and recorded in the old church register:

> 1644. Soldiers slaine 9, August 3.
> And more 5, August 4.
> And 1, August 6.
> And 2, August 8.

Records do not say what most of the villagers were doing during this engagement, except that one party of men were busily cutting wheat in a field at Hazeldine. To their amazement, cannon balls suddenly began to fly over their heads and they took to their heels in terror.

The name Hazeldine recalls an interesting Redmarley association which is provided by a memorial in the north aisle of the church to Major-General Sir Henry Gee Roberts, K.C.B., H.M. Bombay Army 'who after 40 years of an eminent military and political career and distinguished service in the field during the Indian Mutiny in 1857, for which he received the thanks of both Houses of Parliament, died at his residence in Hazeldine House in this parish October 6, 1860, aged 60 years'. Memorials of this kind are sometimes apt to indulge in fancifully fulsome terms, but General Roberts was indeed a distinguished soldier who was once described by his commanding officer, Sir William Napier, as 'an emergency officer, good in every situation; it was impossible to exceed the boldness and readiness of the support he gave me'. He was also an enlightened administrator. As a young captain during a difficult assignment against a lawless horde of tribesmen 'he used his influence acquired as a daring sportsman and a successful soldier to give to the wretched people about him their first experience of power used for other purposes than tyranny and oppression, and of intelligence directed to protect the right and to punish the wrongdoer'.

Roberts was a Gloucestershire man, and early on in his career he bought Hazeldine in Redmarley as a family house during his furloughs, to settled in when he ultimately retired. It was a comfortable, pleasant country home with a view of the distant Malvern Hills, an ideal place for retirement; but when he left India for good in 1859 he was too broken in health to enjoy it and he died a year later, leaving a wife and a family of two sons and a daughter. During the times he had returned to Redmarley, the General must surely have seen in the local newspapers an advertisement like this one:

Pianoforte and Music Warehouse, 10 High Street, Worcester.

By appointment to HER LATE MAJESTY QUEEN ADELAIDE.

ELGAR BROTHERS, Pianoforte and Music Sellers, Tuners, Regulators, Repairers, etc., respectfully invite inspection of their carefully-selected stock of Grand, Cottage and Piccolo Pianofortes, for sale or hire. Church Harmoniums with one or two rows of keys from Six Guineas upwards. First-class tuners sent to all parts of the country.

It is more than possible that the General may have employed one of these Mr Elgars to tune his piano, but it is quite impossible even to imagine what he would have thought (or said) if he had been told by some fortune-teller that one day his daughter would marry the son of one of these local tradesmen. Thirty years after her father's death Caroline Alice married Edward Elgar, son of the Worcester piano-tuner and music-dealer W. H. Elgar.

Caroline Alice was only ten years old when her father died, and after a typically stuffy, shielded Victorian upbringing she seemed fated to remain the unmarried only daughter of a widowed mother. Apart from the usual outlets for an able but frustrated spinster of that period, such as charitable works and sedate local social events, Miss Roberts also had occupations of an artistic kind. She wrote a novel, short stories and some verse, and she took a keen interest in music. It was this latter interest which prompted her in her late thirties to become the pupil of a Malvern music teacher, Edward Elgar, and so to change the whole course of her life. Within a few months she was introducing this shy young musician to members of her family, who must have been openly shocked at her obvious affection for someone who was 'only a musician', although admittedly handsome in appearance. In the following year her mother died; Alice Roberts let Hazeldine House and moved into furnished apartments in Malvern to be near Elgar. Her family must have done everything in their power to induce her to break off the duly announced engagement by stressing his wretched prospects as a beggarly music-teacher; by suggesting that he was merely trying to better himself socially and financially; and by hints of the ultimate consequences of marrying a man seven years younger than herself. Alice Roberts herself had absolutely no doubts that this marriage was to be her vocation, and the wedding took place at Brompton Oratory on 8th May 1889.

The bride had indeed found her vocation, and for the next thirty years she devoted herself singly and wholeheartedly to helping, encouraging, shielding and sustaining the composer who was 'to put England, musically speaking, once again on the map'. She gave up a great deal when she married, but perhaps she never really expected such malevolent opposition from her family. One aunt cancelled a considerable legacy which was to have been left to her, and any children the Elgars might have were expressly debarred from receiving any of the Roberts family's inheritance. In later years after his wife's death Elgar wrote bitterly of this 'hate and prejudice' and of his wife's '*awful aunts*' who could allow nothing to descend to any offspring of *mine*'.

About twenty-eight years after their marriage, Alice Elgar paid a nostalgic visit to her old home at Redmarley; by now she was no longer the wife of a provincial musician, but of Sir Edward Elgar, O.M., the foremost British composer. Perhaps like most returns to a scene of former days, this visit was a mistake, because she noted in her diary that trees she had especially loved in the days of her childhood had disappeared from the garden, and there were signs of neglect everywhere. But she fell in love once again with the house, and thought of what might have been done if they could have afforded to live in it when they had married. She even wistfully worked out where Elgar's study might have been.

You pass the entrance to Hazeldine House on the right, shortly after leaving Redmarley for Bromsberrow, and after going by a signpost improbably pointing the way to 'Drury Lane'. The small road continues through rich farming country, which at harvest time is yellow with ripened corn and where pheasants and partridges run fearlessly from hedge to hedge. This seems such secluded countryside that it is something of a shock suddenly to pass over a motorway with its muffled roar of traffic, and then to cross a main road before you come once again to peace at the village church of Bromsberrow. It is true that the throb and clatter can still be faintly heard here, but it seems very far away, and the occasional farm tractor which comes by the church merely accentuates the tranquillity of this twelfth-century building with its massive oak porch, timbered tower and oak-shingled spire. There is no tower-arch inside the church, but a massive beam in its place bears the date 1502, and both nave and chancel have splendid old trussed rafter roofs. One special treasure of the church is kept in the small Yate chapel on the north side. Here in a glass case are two small cavalry flags of the Civil War, surely unique not only because of their age, but also because they were actually carried in battle and belonged to two brothers who fought on opposite sides. One tattered red silk flag bears a Latin inscription meaning GOD WILL DECIDE AND GOD WILL ASSIST; the other is white and proudly proclaims in Latin THE PROTESTANT RELIGION, THE LAWS OF ENGLAND, AND THE FREEDOM OF PARLIAMENT.

There are other things of interest in this chapel. One is some seventeenth-century glass which depicts the perky figures of two notorious outlawed bandits, Adam Bell and William Cloudeslee. They are suitably bearded and are shown against a convincing landscape, dressed as archers—one in brown, the other in grey— and both sporting a jaunty blue feather in their caps. On the walls of the chapel are three memorials which are favourites of mine because, by the sonority of their language and the stately flow of their periods, they so aptly recall the spacious dignity of a past age. The first is a tribute by a sister to a young theological student who died in his twentieth year:

> In this sepulchral chapel is deposited the mortal part of Robert Gorges Dobyns Yate the younger, a Student in Divinity at St. John's College, Cambridge. He was un-tainted with the dissipation of the Age in which he lived:

His principles were honourable, His literary attainments respectable, and had riper Years been permitted to complete His Character He would have been an Ornament to that sacred Profession for which he was a Candidate, and a Credit to the ancient Family whence He descended . . . He was born at Bromesberrow Place on the 5th of April, 1782 and finished a blameless Life at Dingwood Park on Whitsunday, the 6th of June, 1802.

Another is a tribute from a son-in-law to a doctor:

Cleaver Morris Burland of Wootton-under-Edge in this county, M.B., Descended from an antient and opulent family in the county of Somerset . . . His superior natural abilities were adorned with sound learning acquired in a liberal education which was begun at Westminster School and finished at Christ Church Oxford. The goodness of his heart was genuine and in the discharge of his professional duties as a Physician he was punctiliously exact in his attention to his patients at the expense of his own health and comfort and ever benevolently considerate to the wants of the poor.

The third recalls the memory of a thirteen-year-old child, Annabella-Christiana Yate:

Having loved her with the tenderest affection and considered her as their adopted child, the Rev. Robert Foote and Anne his wife have erected this tablet to her memory. The Vivacity of her Understanding was only equalled by the Purity and Innocence of her Mind. Cherishing the fond Hope of witnessing the fruit of so fair a blossom they could not but bitterly lament a loss which they felt to be all their own.

On the south wall of the chancel there is a much older brass which is more quaintly worded:

Eliza Stock.
Here lies the corpes of her that's wrapt in clay
Whose fame with soule shall also live for aye
While she was sick with sob with sigh with groane
To God Almighty she did make her moane
The help of God was only hir request
So now we hope hir soule in Heaven doth rest.

The road from Bromsberrow to Eastnor is one of the most attractive in this part of Malvern country. It is a winding lane passing through unspoilt rural England at its best, with tall hedges, billowing fields of corn and swelling waves of wooded hills against the background of the Malverns. Here are names that come from the past—names like Pepper Mill and Howler's Barn, Little Woolpits and Joiner's Cottage; and there is even a small brook to be forded. Then the lane widens into a broader road, and the obelisk on high ground above Eastnor Park rises bleakly against the skyline.

Eastnor has its pleasant village features, including thatched black-and-white cottages which should be seen at dahlia time when their gardens are a vivid blaze of colour. There is also a small village green with what was once a handsome drinking-fountain enclosed by a timber and brick canopy decorated with a terracotta panel, representing the scene of Christ and the Samaritan Woman at the well. Unfortunately, like so many other gifts inherited from a former age, this is now badly defaced and neglected. The well water no longer flows and, when I last saw it, rubbish filled the entrance.

The church is rather dim with stained-glass religious light, and the medieval tower is almost all that is left of the original building after Sir Gilbert Scott's drastic restoration of a century ago, but it is certainly worth a visit to see the radiant dignity of the alabaster tomb of the second Earl Somers. There are other treasures here too—a Breeches Bible, several fine oil paintings and two small inlaid chests of Italian workmanship, one with lively figures of knights at the jousts.

It is the castle, of course, which provides the main centre of attraction at Eastnor. Its architect, Samuel Smirke the designer of the British Museum, was obviously given a free hand for this commission, and he certainly produced an imposing and convincing nineteenth-century reconstruction of a crenellated castle of the Middle Ages with four round towers enclosing a central keep. Its impressive dignity has the advantage of a spectacular setting at the edge of a large lake. In 1817, before it was completed, Chambers had visited this newcomer to the great country houses of the district, and the measured phrases of his enthusiastic description seem a fitting background for this dignified building which was begun during the year of Napoleon's disastrous retreat from Moscow, and continued while this country was at deadly grips with the enemy during the Peninsular War.

It is pleasant to be able to add that Eastnor Castle is open from 2.15 to 6 p.m. on Bank Holidays and Sundays from June to September inclusive, so that the public can enjoy the magnificence of its setting and gaze at some of its valuable paintings, tapestries and furniture. Here is a mansion which has not been converted into municipally owned flats, or council offices; nor become the headquarters of a gas board or the administrative centre of a technological university. It is still an English castle, and we should be grateful that in these drab days when everything is done to discourage it there has been enough faith in the future to try to preserve here what the 'progressivists' must regard as an irritating anachronism—a great country house, that last survival of the order, dignity and beauty of a vanished age and a vanished England.

Ledbury may be regarded as the capital of the country west of the Malverns, just as Upton is the capital of the eastern district. There are times when this Herefordshire market town seems almost too good to be real; when it looks for all the world like a particularly convincing theatrical set of a medieval English scene. It is 'a place for half-way seasons and half-lights, for early spring and late autumn, for dawn and nightfall', for then all that is modern seems merged in the overall impression of half-timbered, black-and-white, many-gabled buildings which, like Dickens's Maypole Inn 'with overhanging stories, drowsy little panes of glass, and front bulging out and projecting over the pathway', look as if they were nodding in their sleep. Apart from the general impression of a Tudor backcloth, there are several outstanding individual buildings which give Ledbury its unique character. One of the oldest and most picturesque lurches over the street with its upper story supported on pillars. The seventeenth-century Market House, similarly held up by no less than sixteen impressive solid chestnut supports, cut down from the old Malvern Forest, is one of the sights of the town. So too is the enchanting little cobbled Church Lane with its strip of sky showing above the overhanging gables, and a view of the church at the end. There is a magnificent Elizabethan house, now called Ledbury Park, standing along two sides of a corner with unexpectedly extensive gardens at the rear. The ancient almshouse of St Katherine's Hospital opposite the Market House has a foundation dating back to the thirteenth century, but it was rebuilt in the nineteenth century to the design of Eastnor Castle's architect, Samuel Smirke. The more picturesque view of these modern buildings is from the back, and there are still an ancient dining-hall and chapel to be seen.

Katherine Audley is the patron saint of the town. She was a cousin of the luckless King Edward the Second who was kept overnight in Ledbury as a prisoner during the journey to his grisly end at Berkeley Castle. In a dream she was told to settle in a town where bells should ring a welcome to her by themselves without the agency of human hands. After much wandering, she and her attendant Mabel at last arrived at Ledbury, and as she entered the town the famous bells of the parish church did mysteriously peal out without their ringers. St Katherine had found her home at last, and here she built a hermitage, and lived on an annuity granted to her by her kinsman the King in recognition of her piety and good works. Her story captured the interest of Wordsworth when he was staying in the district and inspired one of his sonnets.

ST CATHERINE OF LEDBURY.

When human touch (as monkish books attest)
Nor was applied nor could be, Ledbury bells
Broke forth in concert flung adown the dells,
And upward, high as Malvern's cloudy crest;
Sweet tones, and caught by a noble lady blest
To rapture! Mabel listened at the side
Of her loved mistress: soon the music died,
And Catherine said, Here I set up my rest.
Warned in a dream, the Wanderer long had sought
A home that by such miracle of sound
Must be revealed: she heard it now, or felt
The deep, deep joy of a confiding thought;
And there, a saintly Anchoress, she dwelt
Till she exchanged for heaven that happy ground.

St Katherine figures in yet another story connected with Ledbury. She is said to have warned the townsfolk not to open the door of the chapel dedicated to her memory in the church. If they waited until it opened itself, Ledbury would become one of the richest towns in the country; if it was opened by human hands the place would sink into poverty. For some time the people of Ledbury waited patiently for the miraculous opening, but one night a riotous party of drunken men stormed into the church and flung the fateful door wide open, and so the town lost for ever its promise of riches. In spite of this calamity Ledbury still looks comfortably prosperous.

The parish church of St Michael and All Angels is one of the seven Herefordshire churches with a tower separate from the main building. It has been suggested that a tower thus detached from the church provided a much more effective defence during the turbulent times of this uneasy district on the borderland, which was always prepared for an attack by the Welsh. The church is a fine building of almost cathedral-like proportions with a variety of styles, ranging from a Norman west door and choir to Decorated work in the baptistery, and a Perpendicular nave. It stands, too, in a peaceful setting reminiscent of a miniature cathedral close. It is impossible here to do more than mention just a few of its more interesting features, and any visitor would be well advised to read the detailed description of this magnificent church in the well-written official booklet which gives its history and a description of its architecture.

For myself I return to the church again and again to look at the baptistery, and at a select half-dozen of the church's splendid collections of monuments which belong to various periods and which are each in its own way outstanding. The Chapel of St Katherine, now used as a baptistery, is a dazzling vision of beauty, especially on a day of sunshine when you can see, set off to perfection, the almost bewildering profusion of the delicate ball-flower ornamentation decorating the windows; the intricate tracery of the windows themselves; and the radiant colours of the medieval glass in its south-west window. As for the monuments, I choose the following six:

1. The remarkably well-preserved effigy of a priest, set upright in the south wall of St Katherine's Chapel; he has an other-worldly saintliness of bearing, subtly suggested even in its black marble.

2. In the North Chapel the elaborate canopied recumbent figure of a woman in flowing robes which is traditionally, although not historically, regarded as that of St Katherine herself.

3. The memorial on the east wall of the same chapel to Edward Moulton Barrett set up by his daughter Elizabeth Barrett Browning, eleven years after her runaway love-marriage with the poet,

for which her father never forgave her. In the circumstances the tablet seems a charitable offering; it shows Barrett on his deathbed (presumably still obdurate against Elizabeth) awaited at the top of a heavenly staircase by angels obviously about to usher him into Paradise.

4. The well-known Skynner memorial in the chancel. This massive piece of marble and alabaster shows the father and mother kneeling, and the more crudely carved figure of their infant child between them. Below are ranged their five other daughters and five sons, and with meticulous attention to detail the third son, a priest, is fittingly shown without a sword and wearing a cassock.

5. The railed-in monument to a husband and wife of the Biddulph family. The reclining figures of the couple are remarkably lifelike in the way they seem to avoid looking at each other. She stares coldly ahead, and he turns aside with a sour expression of ineffable disdain.

6. The loveliest memorial of this church, and perhaps one of the loveliest of any church, is near the Skynner tomb. It is the sleeping figure of eleven-months-old John Martin guarded by two angels. The details of this moving tribute to a small child are of rare excellence, and the sculpture was exhibited at the Great Exhibition of 1851 as an outstanding nineteenth-century work of art.

A sword and some bullets prised out of the west door of the church are preserved in a glass case in St Katherine's Chapel, and recall the battle of Ledbury which took place during the Civil War. In April 1645 the town was held by the Roundhead General Massey with a force of a thousand men. Hearing this, Prince Rupert, who was marching to Shrewsbury from Hereford, turned back with his cavalry and infantry and made a surprise attack on the Parliamentarians at Ledbury. The Cavaliers charged down the long street and, in Prince Rupert's own words, 'Massey was soundly beaten, his foot were quite lost, and his horse beaten and pursued to within six miles of Gloucester'. In the engagement, the Parliamentarian Major Backhouse was mortally wounded and was carried into a house at the Upper Cross where he died. This sword of his was then hidden in the roof of the house where it remained undiscovered for nearly two and a half centuries. The

story of the battle is told in vigorous detail by W. S. Symonds in
the novel *Hanley Castle*:

Ledbury lies pleasantly on the left bank of the river
Leadon, and above it rise the wooded rocky hills of Dog Hill
and the Frith, while on the right, a little more than a mile
distant, is the famous Roman encampment, Wall Hills. The
town consists of one long street leading from the Hereford
and Leominster roads to the Gloucester highway, crossed at
right angles by another shorter street leading from Ross to
Malvern. The old church, with its detached tower and fine
spire, stands a little distance from the town, and a market-
house stands in the wide irregular market-place, much used
in bygone days for baiting bulls, bears and Redmarley
badgers.

Massey was engaged in holding a court-martial upon one
of Prince Rupert's soldiers whom he intended to hang as a
spy, when he was startled by our trumpets as we entered the
Homend on the Hereford road. No time was lost by the
Governor of Gloucester in endeavouring to raise a barricade
of carts and baggage waggons across the Homend where
the street leads to the market-place.

Lord Ashley and Colonel Washington were ordered to
force this barricade with their foot soldiers that we might act
with our cavalry. They cleared a passage in gallant style after
a short half hour's struggle. Lord Loughborough's troop of
horse now charged and we followed close behind. Five
bullets passed through Prince Rupert's clothes and struck
his armour, but he escaped unwounded. It was a fearful
struggle in the open space, with no attempt at strategy, and
my horse, shot through the forehead, fell dead and I fell with
him, hopelessly entangled for the time with the gear and
stirrups. I was partly stunned and found myself lying on the
ground. Then came a rush of our men and I was on my
legs again.

The sound of heavy firing made us aware of a sharp
contest in the direction of the church. I therefore called upon
some men to follow me and ran up the Church Lane. Fierce
fighting was now going on in the churchyard and a number
of the Roundheads fled for shelter to the church itself.
Hoping to prevent bloodshed within the sacred edifice I
entered with a score of Royalists and proclaimed quarter in a
loud voice to all who would lay down their arms, so the
Roundheads withdrew within the large chancel and into the

beautiful chapel of Saint Katherine. An officer of the Parliament now came forward offering to surrender and we discussed the terms briefly, as we stood by the side of that mysterious tomb of some royal lady, that monument of ancient days, bearing the arms of England but which neither by time or date reveals the secret as to the corpse which rests beneath it.

A furious contest now raged in High Street and Southend. Prince Rupert and Massey engaged in a hand-to-hand conflict, and both had their horses shot under them. The struggle continued in the narrow alley called Back Lane and in Bye Street. Here fell Major Backhouse and Captain Kyrle. At last the Parliamentarians gave way and the infantry fled to the neighbouring woods for shelter. Massey, mounting a trooper's horse, galloped down the Gloucester road, followed by as many horses as could clear the town. Giles Nanfan rode in pursuit and chased the rebels four miles.

It was a sorry sight when the fight was over, Englishmen rolling in blood on the ground and clutching the dust in their agony. Opposite the Market-Place sat Honeywood Yates of Bromsberrow, supporting the head of his brother who was apparently dying.[1] The tears streamed down the cheeks of poor Honeywood as he tried to pour some wine into the closed lips of the wounded man whom he had himself struck down in the melée at the barricade. Fortunately the wound was not mortal, and I helped to carry him into the Plume of Feathers, but it was some time before Honeywood recovered from the deadly sickness that came over him when he believed he was a fratricide.

As W. S. Symonds recalls, in the bad old days Ledbury market square often resounded with the shouts and jeers from the spectators of bull-baiting shows, and in his other novel, *Malvern Chase*, there is a graphic reconstruction of this one-time favourite English sport:

We did not find the Bishop at Ledbury but many of his attendants and the neighbouring gentry and clergy had assembled for bull-baiting in the market-place. The bulls were to be baited near the market house, and we indulged our curiosity and watched this national pastime. We joined the committee appointed to see fair play for the bull, as far

[1] *See* page 122.

as fair play could be obtained for a tethered animal. It was determined that only one dog should be loosed at a time, and not three or four as would sometimes be done if the mob had their own way, and the bull proved too good for the dogs. Also we insisted on a fair length of rope and gearing, which the dog owners were apt to make over-short, and thus hardly allow a bull room to turn and meet his savage antagonists. We would not sanction any worrying of bulls by dogs let loose at the close of a baiting, as had been done several times of late to the disgrace of the managers, and was altogether contrary to the rules of the sport.

When we arrived at the ring we found the bull already tethered and fastened by a good rope and leathern girdles across the shoulders and round the neck; but Calverley having measured the rope, we called upon the judges to increase the length by two yards.

The first bull was the largest, and though wild and savage was somewhat unwieldy, so some of the younger dogs were matched against him, and very short work he made with most of them, goring some, trampling others, while two he actually tossed into the middle of the excited crowd. At last a Redmarley dog, well known for his courage and power, was let loose at the now infuriated animal who rushed round the ring, mad with pain and fury. The dog at once pinned the beast by the nose, and notwithstanding his struggles held on until the bull fell exhausted and was declared defeated by the umpires.

The second bull was a much smaller animal, but as active as a cat, and a dark red beast with sharp straight horns. The Redmarley dog was let loose at him, and being somewhat bow-legged and slow, was caught by his horns and killed on the spot. John now came forward with 'Saxon', a tawny dog with great width of chest and an enormous head, 'Saxon', however, fared no better, being met by the bull in full charge and tossed nearly into the street. So powerful, however, was the animal's charge that the rope snapped close at his neck and set him free in the midst of an affrighted crowd. We all ran away, some rushing into Saint Katherine's Hospital, others into houses, and some up the narrow streets leading to the church.

Ledbury is proud to be the birthplace of the Poet Laureate, the late John Masefield, and the town provides the background for parts of his three best-known poems, *The Everlasting Mercy*, *The*

Widow in the Bye Street and *The Daffodil Fields*. The parishioners of Ledbury still gratefully recall, too, that the profits of the poet's *The Ledbury Scene* and *Saint Katherine of Ledbury* were given to the fund for the restoration of their church bells. In *Grace before Ploughing*, John Masefield himself has recalled with nostalgic tenderness the Ledbury of his early childhood days. He writes of the small-sized cobblestones which hurt small feet; of the timber wagons which went past Bye Street into the market-place to the sound of fiercely cracking whips; of the evil-smelling tanneries in Church Lane; of the church itself and its peal of bells; of the busy forge on the Ross road; and of Marcle away in the distance with the Black Mountains of Wales rising behind. Most vivid of all are the recollections of the Ledbury October fair when the broad main street was crowded with booths and cattle pens and the air was filled with the noise of an exhilarating tumult. This fair indeed was the great event which one small boy waited for 'with hope and rapture all the year round'.

About three miles north-east of Ledbury in the parish of Colwall is the estate of Hope End where Elizabeth Barrett Browning spent her early years. For most people her name is more readily associated with London and Florence; and her life story with her famous runaway marriage with Robert Browning, the subject of Rudolph Besier's popular play, *The Barretts of Wimpole Street*, which, appropriately enough, was first produced at the Malvern Festival in 1930 under the direction of Sir Barry Jackson. It was, however, in the shadow of the Malvern Hills that she spent the most impressionable, formative years of her life, and her memories of this happy childhood and of the family home at Hope End inspired some of her most characteristic poetry.

She was only a child of three when her father Edward Moulton Barrett bought the Hope End estate. He had the mansion pulled down, and in its place built a remarkable house of oriental design 'crowded with minarets and domes, and crowned with metal spires and pinnacles', to say nothing of 'Moorish' windows and 'Turkish-style' turrets. It was a place of some size and grandeur, with a suite of reception rooms, a score of bedrooms, plenty of stained glass and a large organ in its spacious, domed entrance hall. Unfortunately this splendid example of Victorian bizarrerie is no longer standing, and the present Hope End is a much more

sober conventional country house, but the fine trees and the
beautiful setting are still there.

A family of twelve children grew up around the formidable Mr
Barrett at Hope End, but Elizabeth was always his favourite child,
and he did everything to encourage her precocious intelligence.
When she grew somewhat older she was given a large room of
her own, 'a lofty chamber with a stained-glass window casting
lights across the floor and upon little Elizabeth as she used to sit
propped against the wall, with her hair falling all about her face, a
childlike fairy figure'. Her precocity was certainly extraordinary.
She read fluently and avidly at the age of five; at eight she could
read Homer in the original 'with book in one hand and doll in the
other'; at twelve she tackled metaphysics, and Locke, Hume and
Voltaire.

Luckily she had some open-air interests as well. She always
retained vivid memories of Hope End and the countryside
around it which she later set down in verse:

> Green the land is where my daily
> Steps in jocund childhood played,
> Dimpled close with hill and valley,
> Dappled very close with shade;
> Summer-snow of apple blossoms running
> up from glade to glade.
>
> Far out, kindled by each other,
> Shining hills on hills arise,
> Close as brother leans to brother
> When they press beneath the eyes
> Of some father praying blessings from
> the gifts of paradise.
>
> While beyond, above them mounted,
> And above their woods also,
> Malvern Hills, for mountains counted
> Not unduly, loom a-row—
> Keepers of Piers Plowman's visions
> through the sunshine and the snow.

Riding was her favourite outdoor occupation, and this was the
cause of an accident when she was about fifteen which affected her
health for the remainder of her life. Impatient at the late arrival of

a groom from the stables, she set out for the meadow and tried to saddle the pony by herself. The animal reared up and Elizabeth fell heavily with the saddle, injuring her back. This made her even more the cherished favourite of the family, and especially of her father. Joseph Arnould has described Edward Moulton Barrett as 'one of those tyrannical, arbitrary, puritanical rascals who go sleekly about the world, canting Calvinism abroad, and acting despotism at home', but Elizabeth has painted a different picture of him with his 'elastic spirit and merry laugh'. There is no doubt about her deep affection for him, and of course we are not bound to accept Rudolph Besier's suggestion of an incestuous streak in the father's love for her: it is a suggestion which appears wholly without any reliable supporting evidence.

It seemed inevitable that such a precocious child should write verse, and at the age of eleven she had produced *The Battle of Marathon* in four books, which the proud father had privately printed with its dedication to himself: 'To him to whom "I owe the most", and whose admonitions have guided my youthful muse, even from her earliest infancy, to the Father whose never-failing kindness, whose unwearied affection, I never can repay, I offer these pages as a small testimony of the gratitude of his affectionate child.' Nine years later when she had made something of a name for herself as a young poet, tragedy struck the Barrett family at Hope End. First Mrs Barrett died suddenly while on a visit to Cheltenham; then came a disastrous change in Mr Barrett's fortunes. His financial affairs fell into confusion; Hope End was put up for sale, and to the agonized distress of Elizabeth prospective buyers tramped through the rooms of their beloved home. At last the furniture was put into store at Ledbury, and the family left for Sidmouth until another permanent home could be found.

For Elizabeth it was the end of a happy childhood, and she never returned to this well-remembered part of Malvern country. 'Beautiful, beautiful hills they are; the Malvern Hills—the hills of *Piers Plowman's Vision* seem to me my native hills, for I was an infant when I first went into their neighbourhood, and I lived there until I had passed twenty by several years,' she wrote long afterwards from the stifling confinement of her sick-room in Wimpole Street. 'And yet not for the whole world's beauty would I stand among the sunshine and shadow of them any more; it would be a mockery, like the taking back of a broken flower to its stalk.'

From Ledbury to Colwall a small winding road signposted to Coddington and Bosbury climbs up and down, giving fine views of the western slopes of the Malverns, with the Herefordshire Beacon towering impressively and clearly showing the encircling rings of its ancient entrenchments. Where the road goes on to Old Colwall take the turning to Colwall, and at the railway bridge bear left and continue to the church along a road which in high summer is heavy with the scent of meadow-sweet, bright with willowherb and loosestrife and colourful with innumerable yellow-hammers.

It is the old part of the parish of Colwall which is scattered around the church, and the nearby Park Farm on the north-west side of the churchyard was once the ancient local residence of the bishops of Hereford, used by them when they came hunting in their section of the forest, or when they were travelling through the diocese. The church has a fine sixteenth-century timbered porch placed rather awkwardly beside the tower. Inside, the timber roof of the nave and the dignified Jacobean pulpit with its fine canopy immediately strike the eye, but there are two other even more interesting things to be seen. One is a beautiful Elizabethan brass on the south wall of the south aisle, showing Anthony Harford and his wife, with six sons ranged behind him, and four daughters behind her, bearing the words:

Here lyeth buryed the body of Elisabeth Harford the wyfe of Anthoni Harford of Bosnuri Esquure, which Elisabeth departed this world the X day of July 1590.

In the wall of the north aisle is a thirteenth-century encaustic tile, obviously from the monastic tile-works at Great Malvern Priory. It pictures a man digging, and it is clearly one of a series representing the months of the year. Probably this one represents March, that time of the year which drives all good gardeners outdoors with their spades.

An interesting glimpse of seventeenth-century Colwall is given in a manuscript now in the British Museum. The *Newe Metamorphosis of J(ervis) M(arkham)* describes in doggerel verse his travels through England in 1600 and his arrival at Colwall. He attended a service at the church and his puritan susceptibilities were much shocked by what he saw there.

> I will relate, from untruth they be free
> Neere to thouse Hilles I did one Saboth kepe
> As good have bin in bed and fast asleepe,
> Oh howe they doe profane the Saboth here.
> I doe protest it made me quake with feare
> For popish superstition they doe still imbrace
> Whereby Religion they doe quite deface.
> They have their Church-Ale and old popish guise,
> Mother of errors and of monstrous lyes.
> The neighbours townes, they on the Saboth feaste,
> A Master of Misrule enterteynes the guest
> With drums and bagpipes and with warlike guns.

He goes on to describe an unusual feature of this Colwall church service. About half way through it parson and congregation broke off and hurried over to the church ale-house which still stands east of the churchyard. They went 'Not to carouse, say they, but to break their fast, Because by then calves-heads will not longer last.'

When the service was finally over they once more made their way to the ale-house, but this time they are unashamedly thirsty in a good cause, for in those days the recognized method of raising funds for the church was by brewing beer to sell at a profit. The disapproving visitor noted that a maypole had already been set up for later jollification, and the rector stumbled through the reading of a 'brief' with great difficulty, partly owing to his illiteracy and partly perhaps owing to the strength of the church ale.

Colwall has developed and spread east of the church right up the slopes of the Malverns, but the curious old Colwall Stone (or its replacement) is in this part of the village not far from the station where trains have emerged from the remarkable tunnel, nearly a mile long, which has been blasted through the rock under the hills.

Colwall is the home of a flourishing branch of the famous firm of Schweppes which settled here towards the end of last century, but you would never suspect that the entrance to the former country house, 'Dilkush', leads to a highly organized factory. 'Dilkush' itself is used for the administrative offices of the branch, and near by is 'The Springs' factory which produces all the carbonated waters. The spring which supplies all the water used in the factory has its source in a rock below the foot of the

Herefordshire Beacon on the north side of the A 449 road shortly before it is joined by Jubilee Drive at the British Camp Hotel. The site is of course private property, but through the kindness of the branch manager, Mr George Honour, I recently had an opportunity of seeing how this spring is piped into a main holding tank of twenty-two thousand gallons, about the size of a small swimming-pool. Strict precautions are taken to maintain the characteristic purity of the Malvern water; the spring itself is enclosed in a small building, and the holding tank is similarly protected so that the limpidity of the water shows up as an almost startlingly pellucid blue.

From here the water is piped for about two and a half miles to 'The Springs' factory, not in a straight line but making an occasional diversion to conform with certain proprietory land rights which existed when the pipes were first laid. One typically English unwritten gentleman's agreement still survives from this period and is regularly honoured three times a year when the Schweppes Malvern water spring fills the swimming-bath of The Elms preparatory school in return for the right to maintain the pipes passing through part of its land. Those with a taste for figures may like to know that the spring at its maximum has a flow of about forty gallons a minute; at its lowest it has fallen to ten gallons a minute, but not even during a drought has it been known to cease altogether.

The isolated little village of Mathon lies beautifully cradled between folds of the hills about two and a half miles north of Colwall, where the Malverns sink down to the plain with enfolding waves of wooded green slopes. Here, as in so many other parts of Herefordshire, there are orchards and hopyards, and in former days the 'Mathon Whites' variety of hops was famous for its fine quality. Francis Brett Young's Benedictine monk Brother John de Mathon[1] would have known the church here in its primitive Norman state when he was a youth and when as he says,

> Little I recked
> Of the realm's turmoil, or the march and counter-march
> Of turbulent barons; for mine own earth was bounded
> By the enfolding hills, and was no larger
> Than the sweet-smelling cowslip-balls we made
> In the meadows of Malvern Chase.

[1] Francis Brett Young, *The Island.*

The east end of the church, with its two lancets and a round window cut through the thick wall, is still an unusually perfect example of original Norman style, and the seven-bayed roof of the nave is a specially fine specimen of fourteenth-century timber work. On the north side of the sanctuary is a seventeenth-century tomb which was obviously moved here at some later date, as the inscription is now against the east wall and cannot be seen. The effigies are of Jane Walweyn, her husband John and their tiny child; the carving is so clearly cut and so remarkably preserved that it is difficult to believe that it was done three and a half centuries ago.

On the same wall is a memorial to Mary Cliffe which tenderly records:

> She was: but words are wanting to say what:
> Say; she was Vertuous, Good, and she was that.

There are three other eighteenth-century epitaphs here which deserve recording. One is on the left of the timbered porch and is to the memory of John Barrett with the words:

> You that are young prepare to die,
> For I am young tho here I lie,
> My Pain was Gret before I did,
> My Life was crav'd but God den'd.

The second is in the tower chamber and commemorates Joseph Bonaeale, yeoman, with these solemn words:

> For many days my Friends did see
> Approaching Death attending me,
> No favour could this Body have
> Till it was laid within the Grave.
> All you that are Spectators here
> Prepare for Death for it draws near.

The third is on the floor of the nave just below the chancel step. It is a diamond-shaped stone with the words:

> Here
> lyeth ye Body
> of ELIZ: CLIFFE,
> wife of ALLEN CLIFFE
> Esqr. Died June 5th 1754,
> Aged 78; Who desired
> never to be remov'd
> by humane
> Hands.

Even in a county well known for its bells, Mathon is acknowledged to have a particularly fine peal of six, together with a Sanctus bell which were all cast in Gloucester, the six by Rudhall in 1760, and the Sanctus by Martin nearly a century before. All six of the peal have inscriptions:

1. The Treble F: *Peace and Good Neighbourhood*
2. The E flat: *Prosperity to the Town*
3. The D flat: *God preserve our Church and State*
4. The C: *Fear God, Honour the King.*
5. The B flat: *Glory to God*
6. The Tenor A flat: *The Living to the Church I call*
                      And to the Grave I summon all.

Campanologists will be interested to know that on Boxing Day, 1951, a peal of 5040 Minor (one extent of Oxford Treble Bob, and two extents each of Kent Treble Bob and Plain Bob) was rung in two hours and forty-nine minutes.

An old board here proclaims some eighteenth-century 'Rules for Ringers':

> Ye gentlemen ringers both far and near,
> That are disposed for to ring here;
> Observe this law, and mark it well;
> The Man that Overthrows his Bell,
> Six-pence he to the Clark must pay,
> Before that he go hence away,
> If he Ring with Glove, Spur, or Hat,
> Six-pence he must pay for that.
> If he either Curse or Swear,
> Six-pence he must pay while you are here,
> This is not a place to Quarrel in,
> To Curse, and Swear, it is a Sin.

Cradley is a mile farther north, and like Mathon it is situated below the folds of wooded billowing slopes sinking down from the Malverns. There are some pleasant black-and-white timbered houses in the village, and one of special interest stands at the south-east corner of the churchyard. Over five centuries old, it was formerly a school for boys but now does duty as the parish hall. Although the village itself is tucked in a green leafy hollow, the church stands on a ridge above it. It has a fine old lych-gate and a massive square tower supported inside by giant oak timbers, but I personally find equally impressive the nine-foot length of the great parish chest at the back of the church, cut out of a single tree trunk and fitted with no less than five locks.

There are two modern features of Cradley church which I think excellent. Firstly, most of the ancient upright tombstones have been preserved, but they are carefully and neatly set against the churchyard walls so that the turf can be kept well trimmed. Secondly, some ugly yellow Victorian glass has been replaced by clear panes, some with an inserted inscription as a memorial. And if you go to Cradley church you will enjoy the east window with its figure of St Francis surrounded by rabbits and birds; and you will appreciate the memorial sundial in the churchyard with its inscription:

'THYME TRYETH TROTH.'

From Cradley you join the main road A 4103 to return to Great Malvern, but at Storridge you can make an interesting detour by turning left to Birchwood. Here in the peaceful surroundings of great beauty, and within sight of the hills they both loved so well, Elgar and his wife had a small cottage during the important Malvern stage of his career. Birchwood Lodge is now a farm; it has been much altered, and its setting is obviously much less wooded than formerly, but it is still possible to picture it as it was seventy years ago, remote and half hidden by trees. Elgar once said to Basil Maine that before he could write real music he had to be 'quiet and apart', and this cottage was a cherished get-away from the musical chores, interruptions and distractions of Malvern. 'Just leaving for Birchwood. Deo Gratias,' he wrote to his close friend, Jaeger. 'Saturday, date and month and year unknown 'cos it's Birchwood. We climb down to the valley on Wdy. a.m. I cuss every step away from these woods.' And during a very hot August: 'I don't like to say a word about these woods for fear you should feel envious, but it is godlike in the shade with the snakes and other cool creatures walking about as I write my miserable music.'

The score of *The Dream of Gerontius* is inscribed 'A. M. D. G. Birchwood. In Summer, 1900', and it was in this small cottage that much of the great music of that oratorio was scored. In her

book *Edward Elgar, Memories of a Variation*, Mrs Richard Powell
recalls a visit she paid to Birchwood on a very hot summer day.

> I had bicycled from Wolverhampton, forty miles, and
> arrived, rather warm and dusty at the cart-track leading up
> through the woods to the house. When I was nearly there I
> thought I would rest, out of sight, and get cool. I heard the
> piano in the distance, and not wishing to lose more of it than
> I need, I soon went on. In a moment I came in sight of the
> Lady [1] sitting on a fallen tree just below the windows. She
> had a red parasol. I think she sat there partly to warn people
> off—particularly people with bicycles who had been known
> to commit the awful crime of ringing a bell to announce their
> arrival. Leaning the bicycle against a tree, I went and sat
> down by her without speaking. He was playing the opening
> of Part II of *Gerontius*, and those who know the music well
> will understand what it was like to hear that strangely aloof,
> ethereal music for the first time in such surroundings. Each
> time I hear it I think of that beautiful place and that glorious
> day with the sunshine coming through the lace-work of
> greenery and branches and the deep-blue sky over all.

As W. H. Reed remarked many years later when he visited the
cottage with Elgar, 'it seemed such an ordinary cottage until I
was overcome and not a little awed by the knowledge of what had
come out of it'.

[1] Elgar's wife.

CHAPTER NINE

Malvern Today

ALTHOUGH quite a number of people still do have the good sense
to retire there, Malvern is of course no longer only a last retreat of
retired colonels or a haven for elderly ladies in private hotels.
Malvern is now a lively place with a busy life and a distinctive
character of its own; it is not dependent upon tourists for its
money, but earns its own living and spends its own income in its
own way. One characteristic feature of the town is that its age
group, at least during term time, is considerably affected by one of
its 'main industries'—private schools. Apart from Malvern
College, and Malvern Girls' School (the order is chronological),
I have counted at least seven private boys' schools and no less than
five private girls' schools in Malvern and district. The result of
this is that there is generally a healthy leaven of youth in Malvern,
and a continuous infusion of young temporary residents who take
away with them memories they have stored up during the most
impressionable years of their lives. During the war, however, a
more permanent influence was felt in the town with the coming
of R.R.E. The Radar Research Establishment as it was then called
was formed in 1953 by the amalgamation of the Telecommunications Research Establishment (T.R.E.) and the Radar Research
and Development Establishment (R.R.D.E.) which was hurriedly
moved to Malvern during the war to avoid the possibility of their
research experiments being within 'listening distance' of the
enemy. As already mentioned in Chapter V, T.R.E. occupied
Malvern College after the boys had been evacuated to Harrow,
and R.R.D.E. moved into new quarters to the north of the
town. In 1957 the Queen visited the establishment, and at her
command the initials R.R.E. now stand for 'Royal Radar
Establishment'.

Both of the original establishments making up R.R.E. grew

out of a team formed before the war in order to develop methods of locating enemy aircraft by radio. When war broke out in 1939 it was fortunate for this country that as a result of their work there was already in existence a chain of twenty stations maintaining a continuous watch here at home, while several had even been installed overseas at certain strategic places. During the war the work done at Malvern was of the utmost importance, and many special applications of radar technique were developed 'for directing searchlights, aiming A.A. guns, aircraft navigation, blind bombing, surface vessel detection, aircraft interception, etc.—and radar played vital roles in the battles of Britain and of the Atlantic, and in the invasion of Europe in 1944'.[1] If, as Wellington is said to have claimed, the battle of Waterloo was won on the playing-fields of Eton, then we can certainly accept that the Battle of Britain was won on the playing-fields of Malvern.

When the war was over it was recognized that there was a growing need to study electronic materials and devices more fundamentally; a Physics Group was set up at R.R.E., and there is continual development of their research on the highly sophisticated techniques necessitated by the complexities of modern defence systems. R.R.E. is the largest centre for electronics research in the country and one of the largest of all government research establishments. It welcomes inquiries from those who are interested in pursuing a career of research and development in the electronics field which by reason of its basic role in technology is bound to become more and more important in the future. It is pointed out in the official booklet, R.R.E. Offers Opportunities, that 'the research and development programme of R.R.E. offers an almost unique range of exciting work to the scientist. Among the many current activities are infra-red techniques, new ideas in transistor development, high-power valve research, electronic digital computing, micro-wave techniques, very low temperature and solid state physics, techniques associated with lasers, magnetic films and cryotrons, non-linear servo mechanisms, propagation studies, weapon guidance, radio-astronomy and pan-climatic testing.'

The Three Counties Agricultural Show, held on a permanent

---

[1] R.R.E. Offers Opportunities.

site at Blackmore Park Road since 1958, brings another lively scene of bustle and business to Malvern every year during its three days in June. This show, one of the most important of its kind, had its distant origin in the Herefordshire Agricultural Society, which was founded in 1797 with not only such magnanimous motives as 'encouraging industry and fidelity among servants employed in husbandry' and 'rewarding labourers who shall bring up or have already brought up the greatest number of legitimate children without any or with the smallest relief from their respective parishes', but also with the object of encouraging experiments to improve agricultural methods, to try out new implements, to test crops, to improve the breeds of horses, cattle and sheep, and 'in short, to recommend and bring into practice all the means of facilitating labour, of exciting and rewarding industry, and of receiving at the least expense the greatest quantity and the most improved quality of animal and vegetable foods'.

Prizes for the first few shows were 'three silver goblets and the balance in hand was but forty pounds. The subscription list totalled ninety-nine pounds and the membership was only one hundred strong'.[1] These are certainly modest figures compared with the present Three Counties Show's membership of over 4,700, its assets of more than sixty thousand pounds and its annual prizes to the value of some ten thousand pounds.

In 1870 a suggestion was made that the Herefordshire society should join up with other counties, but after a good deal of discussion the committee finally decided against taking such a step. Thirty-four years later, however, changed circumstances effected an amalgamation with the county of Worcestershire, and in 1921 Gloucestershire joined the Herefordshire and Worcestershire Agricultural Society to form the present Three Counties Agricultural Society. For many years the new society held its shows at each of the three county cities in turn, with an occasional visit elsewhere, but the increasing difficulties of finding suitable sites, and the harsh economic facts of rising costs of labour and transport made it imperative to find a permanent site. Finally, with the help of the Malvern Chamber of Commerce, the present site at Malvern Wells was obtained and has proved a happy

[1] Glynne Hastings, *Short History of the Three Counties Agricultural Society*.

choice for the convenience of its position and access, and for the extent of its area which includes several acres of woodland.

The first show to be held on this new permanent site was in 1958, when the society entertained the Queen Mother who was particularly delighted with the magnificent setting and the background of the Malvern Hills. 'The first five-year programme on the site included laying down an adequate road system; installation of permanent electricity, water, telephone and other services, and the building of a permanent office, including a council room, which is used throughout the year for the administration of the society's affairs.

'Over the past eight years the woodland has been gradually developed in co-operation with the Forestry Commission to form a permanent exhibition area where the latest developments in woodland work can be demonstrated. An extensive tree-planting scheme has been undertaken also in the showyard proper which extends for some seventy acres and which now houses stands and displays showing all the latest developments in agriculture, horticulture, education and forestry. The fact that entries both of trade firms and livestock exhibitors continue to rise, and that new members are constantly being enrolled indicates that the future of the society as one of England's premier national agricultural events is assured.' [1]

Besides having for the specialists such exhibits as the principal breeds of British cattle, sheep and pigs, and examples of the latest types of agricultural machinery, this annual show has other attractions—an extensive flower display section, horse-jumping trials, parades of foxhounds, military displays, sheep-shearing competitions, dog obedience trials, tractor and trailer driving competitions, forestry exhibitions, and many other events which attract hundreds of members of the general public as well as those with a special interest in agriculture.

Malvern's healthy situation, educational facilities, geographical position and accessibility by road and rail all make it an ideal centre to develop an industrial estate, and within the past few years the local council has given ready encouragement and assistance to firms wishing to move to the town. About sixteen acres of suitable land at Spring Lane were set aside for sale to

[1] Glynne Hastings, *Short History of the Three Counties Agricultural Society.*

industrialists, and now a number of firms are well established, with industries ranging from toolmaking and precision engineering to plastic mouldings manufacture; and from the making of automatic packaging machinery to 'a documentation service for the preparation of illustrated technical handbooks'. The success of this enterprise has led to an expansion of the facilities offered, and seven acres to the north and eleven acres to the south of the original site have been developed and are occupied by other firms.

Up to now this development, so desirable from a commercial point of view, seems to have been contained within limits set by a proper regard for the unique character of the area. There are some who view the future with some apprehension, however; they fear that the industrial estate may spread still further, to the detriment of Malvern's amenities; but it is to be hoped that those in authority, backed by a strong body of public opinion, will prevent any kind of industrial expansion which would threaten such a precious heritage of conspicuous beauty and historic interest.

Index